Empowered

Pregnancy

The Ten Most Important Things to Know in Pregnancy

THEODORE M. PECK M.D.
& VICKI BENUSA PECK B.S.N.

Web Site: www.FellPub.com

Frederick Fell Publishers, Inc.

2131 Hollywood Boulevard, Suite 305

Hollywood, Florida 33020

954-925-5242

e-mail: fellpub@aol.com

Visit our Web site at www.fellpub.com

Library of Congress Cataloging-in-Publication Data

Peck, Theodore M.
   Empowered pregnancy : the ten most important things to know in pregnancy/ by Theodore M. Peck and Vicki Benusa Peck.
     p. cm.
   ISBN 0-88391-037-3
    1. Pregnancy. 2. Prenatal care. 3. Consumer education. I. Peck, Vicki Benusa. II. Title.

RG524 .P34 2002
618.2'4--dc21

              2001054720

10 9 8 7 6 5 4 3 2 1
Graphic Design: Elena Solis

Acknowledgments

The publication of this book would not have been possible without the help of many kind people, most of whom provided free services gladly given and gratefully received. The bulk of the typing and secretarial work was very ably provided by Jessie Reinhart, without whose services we could not have managed. The illustrations were provided by a very talented Kathy Troyanek.

Being first-time authors, we were frequently in need of direction and encouragement which was effectively given by Dr. Roz Meadow and Bob Golden, both authors themselves. Help has come from many sources: editing from Charlotte Grant and Mary Ann Shah, business and production assistance from Nancy Noelke and Erin Kujak, nursing ideas from Marie Walter and Beth Padesky, and perspective from pregnant couples Dr. Dan and Erin Kujak and Allysen Hoberg and Dan Wiersgalla. The subject of one of our stories, Sue Barnett, was kind enough to allow us to write her story and use her name.

We want to thank our literary agent, Carol Susan Roth, who had the vision to see what this book could become and helped us to make it a reality. And, finally, Elisabeth Bing, Mary Ann Shah, Nancy Noelke, Barb Hammes, Suzanne Arms and Sheila Kitzinger all took time to review the manuscript and we thank them for their efforts and comments.

Dedication

This book is dedicated to Mothers...
Especially my Mother, who teaches strength by example.
V.B.P.

and to Patsy, who
would have been very pleased.
T.M.P.

Table of Contents

Thing to Know: You are in control of all decisions which need to be made about your pregnancy.

Thing to Know: For healthy women expecting an uncomplicated pregnancy, midwifery care is usually the better choice.

Thing to Know: Much of what you are told about pregnancy care is untrue and leads to unnecessary anxiety and suffering.

Thing to Know: Decisions about genetic testing are important and need to be carefully considered.

Thing to Know: There are good ways to relieve or reduce the pain of childbearing.

Thing to Know: Natural delivery is almost always the best method.

Thing to Know: Breastfeeding is significantly healthier for your baby than bottle-feeding.

Introduction

Pregnancy and delivery have never been safer for mothers or babies. Scientific advances in pregnancy care have led to extraordinarily low newborn death rates, and maternal deaths are rare. Unfortunately, in the process of relying on new technology, pregnant women appear to have lost control of their own pregnancies. Decisions are often being made for them by their doctors and the medical care system, leading to increased anxiety and dependence. As a result, maternal dissatisfaction and malpractice suits have increased in direct proportion to the number of times when the expected "perfect" delivery and baby have not materialized.

Physicians' fear of malpractice suits is reflected in a corresponding increase in the cesarean section rate, which has been hovering just below 25 percent for the last ten years.

Obstetric care in America is coming to a natural turning point, as pregnant women are becoming more vocal about their dissatisfaction with the high cesarean rate and the loss of control over their medical care.

In the course of our relationships with thousands of pregnant women, we have identified several concepts and principles that pregnant women need to know. This book is intended to educate and encourage pregnant women to retain control over the decisions and events of their pregnancy and thus get the most out of their medical care during this exciting time.

A historical perspective is helpful. During the first 30 years of the 20th century, the specialty of obstetrics was in its own infancy. Most babies were born at home, and women who had their babies in hospitals were attended to by general practitioners. There was little known about the mysteries of pregnancy, and doctors could provide only the most basic medical support.

Women, at that time, could expect a very natural result to their pregnancies. This was not always a good thing, because newborn death rates were high and occasional maternal deaths were expected. Those women with physician care received little intervention, and the rate of cesarean sections was very low.

In the 1940s, 50s, and 60s, physicians still knew little about the intricacies of pregnancy and delivery, but improved ways to alleviate pain, treat deadly infections, and save women's lives made delivery in hospitals much more appealing. Pain relief in labor was achieved with powerful narcotics, and general anesthesia was frequently used for delivery. This worked well to control pain, but left many newborns limp and in need of resuscitation. Forceps deliveries became the norm. Women often could not remember anything about their own deliveries, and doctors were in such control that laboring women were often strapped to delivery tables. Fathers typically waited in the waiting room, smoking, until they were notified of the delivery results. The rate of cesarean sections was still very low (about 5 percent).

The 1970s ushered in our present obstetric system. Nearly all American babies are now born in hospitals, and an explosion of obstetric knowledge has changed the entire pregnancy experience into a complex scientific project from beginning to end. Fetal heart-rate monitoring has become routine, and frequent medical tests are expected. Epidural anesthesia in labor has replaced the narcotics and general anesthesia of the previous era.

Scientific half-truths, ever-changing data, and the medical system's fear of malpractice suits has resulted in excessive maternal anxiety and a movement away from natural birth and toward an artificially controlled pregnancy. Our goal in writing this book is to help pregnant women get the best of both approaches, natural and scientific. In doing so, they can achieve the best possible pregnancy experience.

Notes to the Reader

In an attempt to minimize gender confusion, we are going to refer to all physicians and babies in masculine terms (he, him, etc.) and to all nurses, midwives, and doulas in feminine terms.

The information and advice in this book is general and cannot be used as a substitute for professional advice in individual circumstances. You should consult your physician or midwife before acting on any of the information presented in this book.

The names, individual traits, and exact details in the stories presented may have been altered to protect privacy while preserving coherence.

Chapter 1

Who is in Control of Your Pregnancy?

When you first become pregnant, you see that your entire world is about to change, not only physically, but emotionally, financially and socially. It is an exciting and yet frightening realization. You naturally have an urgent need to know what you are getting yourself into. The information and medical care you receive during your pregnancy can have a profound effect on you and your baby.

Of all the things you need to know in pregnancy, the most important one is this: *You are in control of all the decisions which need to be made about your pregnancy care and delivery.*

In spite of times when you may feel your pregnancy care is at the mercy of the medical establishment, you can be, in fact, in a position of power. Once you realize this, it becomes clear why this book and its recommendations are so important.

By making decisions that are right for you, in the end you will experience the most significant and memorable event between your own birth and death, and it will be intensely satisfying.

Control

During your pregnancy, who is in charge? You or your doctor? The answer is simple and yet complex. In order for women and their doctors to best deal with the issue of control during pregnancy care, the issues of <u>autonomy,</u> <u>beneficence,</u> and <u>responsibility</u> must be clearly understood.

Autonomy

Autonomy refers to your ability as a competent individual to make decisions about your own welfare and actions. When your doctor respects your autonomy, he is simply treating you as he would like to be treated himself. He gives you information and advice and, most of the time, what he suggests is reasonable, and you agree to his plan.

This respect for autonomy is something that a lot of doctors and nurses, not just obstetricians, have trouble with. We are so used to telling you what is good for your health that we sometimes forget to realize that, while health issues are very important, they are not the only issues in your life.

It is critical for pregnant women to realize the importance and power of their autonomy. Doctors are legally and ethically bound to respect it. For example, your doctor cannot perform a cesarean section on you unless you sign a form permitting him to do so.

Doctors have their own autonomy. They make decisions regarding their own actions as well, and cannot be forced to do surgical procedures or provide medical care they feel is dangerous, inappropriate, unethical, or illegal.

Beneficence

This is the principle of doing more good than harm and it is at the center of all medical care. It affects every medication we prescribe, every operation we perform, every medical plan we devise, and every test we ask our patients to have done to them.

Ideally, physicians should only be thinking of your good or your harm when giving advice or suggesting a course of action. Sometimes, however, that is not the case. Other factors may affect their judgement, such as the amount of their available time, your insurance policy's limitations, their concern about malpractice suits, and their attitudes toward the doctor-patient relationship in general.

Responsibility

Many women do not want decision-making responsibility. By willingly and automatically agreeing to all of their doctor's suggestions, they yield total control and responsibility. This is not a good thing to do, because it makes women more dependent on their doctors. All outcomes, good or bad, become the doctor's accomplishments. Therefore, the pregnant woman feels less satisfied with her normal, healthy delivery, and more angry if she perceives that something went wrong.

Your Doctor's Role

With few exceptions, obstetricians almost always know a great deal more about pregnancy care than their patients do. Unfortunately, nearly all of their training relates to disease and pathology. Very little of their education focuses on the normal, healthy pregnant woman and her needs. As a result, **American obstetric care is primarily directed at identification and treatment of pregnancy-related disorders that occur in only a minority of women.**

Since most pregnant women are healthy and should expect normal pregnancies, vaginal deliveries and healthy babies, this focus on the disorders of pregnancy can detract from the normal positive pregnancy experience.

Your Role

So, let us get back to the original question. Who is in charge during your pregnancy? **Who makes the decisions? You do.**

Your doctor can make suggestions, give advice, pre-scribe medicines, perform procedures, and order tests, but you are the one who is primarily responsible for deciding if you will follow that advice, take the medicines, and have the tests or procedures done. In order to make the right deci-sions, you need to be knowledgeable on the issues, which will give you the self-confidence and assertiveness necessary to say "no", when "no" is your best answer.

Some decisions are more important than others. We make small decisions every day-what to wear, what to eat for breakfast, etc. The same is true about pregnancy care from beginning to end.

During the first obstetrical visit, a complete examination including a pelvic exam is routine. Most women don't like pelvic exams, but <u>decide</u> to submit because the doctor gets valuable information by doing one. Later, the doctor sug-gests doing blood tests. Again, few women like being stuck with needles, but they <u>decide</u> to allow it, so the doctor can get more information which may be helpful.

These are not major decisions, but they are decisions just the same. It is not unusual for a woman to refuse a pelvic exam. It is her right to do so. Some valuable information will not be available, but the doctor can work around it. Sometimes, women don't want to have blood-sugar tests done. This is also their right, and the doctor can work around that too.

Other decisions are more significant and require more thought, knowledge, and discussion. These topics include the induction of labor, epidural anesthesia, vaginal delivery after a previous cesarean section, and breech delivery. Regardless of the suggestions of your obstetrician, the final decision is yours.

From the Nurse's Notes

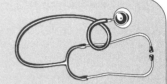

Few doctors realize how difficult it is for their patients to be direct or assertive with them. It would probably surprise most obstetricians to find out that their patients are often so intimidated by them that they are unable to relate many of their needs and desires.

Even the most kind, benevolent, caring, pleasant, and unhurried doctor will unwittingly evoke some apprehension in most patients. It isn't his fault, and it isn't their fault; it is simply normal human nature.

Very often, doctors listen to a patient's complaints when these complaints are not the real problem. Something else, something bigger, something more personal, is troubling her, but she cannot bring herself to overcome her fear and be open enough to discuss it directly.

The insightful physician may recognize this and probe into the matter, eventually getting to the real problem. Unfortunately, most are either not that insightful or do not feel that they have the time to cut through all the extraneous defenses the patient has put up. This problem is all too common in situations involving domestic violence (See Chapter 10.)

To maximize your control during pregnancy:

- Organize and write down your thoughts before your appointment and take them with you.
- Take advantage of the educational brochures in your doctor's office. Quite often, what you want may already be standard procedure for your doctor or hospital.
- Discuss your concerns directly with your doctor.
- Learn about pregnancy. The more you know, the more self-confident you will be. That self-confidence will allow you to be more assertive.
- Being assertive does not mean being aggressive. Be pleasant. Ask his opinion. Keep an open mind.

Approaching your doctor with your concerns and desires may cause you some apprehension. Don't let that keep you from attaining your goal. Self-confidence and assertiveness will help you to determine your care during pregnancy.

Entering the Medical Care System

When you are having your first baby, entering into the medical system can be a confusing and frightening experience. Usually, you get a great deal of advice from female friends and relatives. If you pay attention to this advice, you enter into prenatal care with a scattered amount of information (much of it incorrect) and certain expectations based on other people's experiences.

Of the four million American women expecting babies this year, 90 to 95 percent will seek the care of doctors. Eighty percent of those doctors will be obstetricians. The remaining 5 to 10 percent will either seek care from midwives or avoid prenatal care entirely. Over 99 percent will deliver their babies in hospitals or similar medical care facilities. Fewer than 1 percent of babies are born at home.

The First Prenatal Visit

Regardless of the kind of doctor or midwife you go to, your first prenatal visit will nearly always include filling out a medical and social history questionnaire, a physical exam, and blood tests. You will also receive information in the form of pamphlets or books which you are encouraged to read.

During that first prenatal visit, very important information is shared. You may be asked to reveal many personal medical facts and social details which even your best friends may not know.

You, in return, get information. In addition to the pamphlets, you get a first impression of your doctor and the general medical philosophy you can expect to deal with for the remainder of your pregnancy.

A New Attitude

After your pregnancy is verified, you return to your social circle as a pregnant woman and begin to evaluate your environment quite differently than you did a few months earlier. It is natural to begin to think about eating healthier foods and avoiding those activities, medications, and environmental chemicals which may cause harm to you or your baby.

It is at this point that anxiety begins to build. What is a healthy diet? What foods should I avoid? How can I stay in a totally smoke-free environment? Will sex hurt the baby? Can I get a perm? Can I paint the baby's room? Can I drink coffee? The list of questions may be endless.

> You may read articles in magazines and newspapers about the dangers of some medicines or chemicals in pregnancy and wonder if you have to worry about your baby. Your friends may tell stories about someone's terrible ordeal during labor and how awful a certain doctor or hospital is. You may wonder if this could happen to you.

It is not surprising, given the barrage of diverse opinions, that by the time the average normal, healthy pregnant woman gets well into pregnancy, fear and anxiety become prominent emotions.

These feelings are not limited to the pregnant woman. Doctors, midwives, labor and delivery nurses, pharmacists, hospital administrators, and others in the medical care system also suffer a pregnancy-induced anxiety, only theirs is the fear of being sued for malpractice.

Additionally, the extra testing and precautions prescribed by anxious physicians may lead to an ever-ascending spiral of worry. This scenario reaches its ridiculous peak during labor, when fetal heart-rate monitoring becomes the prime focus of anxiety. Labor and delivery nurses, doctors, and the laboring mother are all riveting their attention on every little blip in the baby's heart rate, instead of focusing on the needs of the laboring mother.

Effects of Anxiety

Pregnancy is naturally a time of concern about the health of the pregnant woman and her baby. To a certain extent, a proper respect and fear of potentially disastrous outcomes is appropriate and healthy. As anxiety increases however, it may lead to a variety of unnecessary problems. Initially, the worst problem is the emotional stress of living in an anxious condition. Typically, it causes a person to lose objectivity. This may make you more willing to do things you would not ordinarily do, (e.g. long-term bed rest, having an operation, and submitting to many medical tests) because dependence on the doctor markedly increases as the level of insecurity rises.

Physically, heightened anxiety results in increased symptoms of heartburn, headache, and insomnia, just to name a few. In labor, anxiety leads to muscle tension, which increases the sensation of pain. It can also result in poor labor progress. (See chapter 6.)

The consequence of all this is an extraordinarily high rate of cesarean sections and forceps deliveries. Today's pregnant woman, often feeling fearful and dependent, may not have sufficient self-confidence or knowledge to be assertive enough to change the course of these events. This may lead to being physically and emotionally manipulated by an over-controlling and under-caring medical system.

The Doctor-Patient Relationship

In the doctor-patient relationship, when communication fails, the patient is the one who suffers. Realizing these things, we can help you break those barriers, bridge the doctor-patient communication gap and thereby improve your pregnancy care and childbirth experience. If pregnancy and delivery are such natural events, why should it

matter if the relationship between the pregnant woman and her doctor is considerably less than satisfactory? The answer is that American pregnancies, for good and bad reasons, are rarely totally natural.

In their efforts to make pregnancy as safe as possible and to make labor and delivery experiences satisfying, doctors have changed pregnancy care from a completely natural process to a highly managed one.

A managed process requires someone to control the many decisions which need to be made. Doctors have transformed portions of pregnancy care, especially labor and delivery, into <u>micro</u>-management. Emotional responses to obstetricians' actions, perceived by mothers-to-be as over-aggressive, insensitive, or inhumane, can be surprisingly intense and long lasting. These situations can be avoided if communication between the doctor and the pregnant woman is open and honest.

From the Doctor's Files

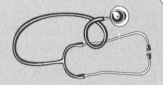

I frequently ask pregnant women who have previously had children about their experiences with other obstetricians. Their comments often reflect the pain and bitterness they felt. Over the years, I have learned from them a great deal about what not to do.

Here are a few examples of the things I've heard:

"There were times when I felt I was being treated like a piece of meat."

"I had an awful lot of exams I didn't want. There was a student and an intern and somebody else. I am a shy person, and it really annoyed me to have to subject myself to all of that."

"I don't even know why I went in for my prenatal visits. The doctor was in and out so fast that I never even got to ask him any questions. All he said was that everything was okay and left."

"The (fetal heart rate) monitor was on me all the time, and I felt like I couldn't move. It was very frustrating and uncomfortable."

All of these comments were from women who did well physically, yet the negative feelings were intense and led them to seek the care of another obstetrician for their next pregnancy.

These women all suffered because of poor communication—theirs, as well as that of their doctors. With more self-confidence and assertiveness, these women could have made a change in how they were treated.

The information in this book can help you increase your self-confidence and knowledge, which will enrich your communication with medical staff. This will improve how you are treated during your pregnancy, labor and delivery.

Many women feel more comfortable seeing a female doctor for their pregnancy care. It may come as a surprise to you though, that female physicians have about the same cesarean and instrument (forceps or vacuum) delivery rate as their male counterparts.

Most relationship problems between a pregnant woman and her doctor could be resolved if the doctor would spend more time with her during prenatal visits and while she is in labor. In order to do so, however, the average obstetrician would have to work many more hours a week. This kind of work load is obviously unreasonable, making a resolution of this problem unlikely if the present system of American obstetric care continues unchanged. Most doctors will not voluntarily reduce the number of patients they see in order to improve the time and quality of care they can offer to an individual. They, or their medical facility, would lose too much money.

If improvement is going to occur in the amount of time pregnant women have with their care-givers, the changes required are going to have to be initiated by pressure from pregnant women themselves. Doctors need an incentive to change the system.

Changing the System

Instead of risking a home delivery or enduring the occasionally oppressive, but safer, physician-controlled care system, you can have the best of both without increased risks to yourself or your baby. There is an achievable alternative, which will serve to balance the safety benefits of modern obstetric care with the emotional benefits of a more "natural" pregnancy.

25

This is how it should work:

You begin by seeing a certified nurse midwife (CNM) who interviews and examines you (See chapter 2). Once it is determined that your pregnancy is at low risk for complications, all further prenatal visits are with the CNM. Pregnant women with medical problems, or at high risk to develop them, are seen primarily by physicians.

Throughout the pregnancy, you are given plenty of time to discuss various concerns, needs, and problems.

You will be encouraged to eat a balanced diet and, by doing so, you can avoid taking daily multiple vitamin pills. You may use designated safe over-the-counter medicines for minor medical problems after the first three months of pregnancy. (See chapter 3.)

A diagnostic obstetric ultrasound is offered at 16 to 20 weeks, and you and your husband (or significant other) can get a good look at your baby. Bring a videotape along so you can take this experience home with you. Fetal genetic testing is offered and discussed in detail after the ultrasound has been completed. You can then decide how you want to deal with this issue. (See chapter 4.)

In mid-pregnancy, the midwife explains the benefits of relaxation techniques, and you might enroll in a program provided by the medical center, which allows you to have a labor and delivery with much less pain and medical intervention. (See chapter 5.) This relaxation program may be based on hypnotherapy, hydrotherapy, massage, or some other relaxation technique. You work on this relaxation program at home periodically for the rest of the pregnancy.

During the course of the pregnancy, the issue of domestic abuse is discussed. Women in dangerous relationships are given information about sources of assistance and ways to deal with their situation. (See chapter 10.)

You begin labor knowing that you are very likely to have a normal delivery. The cesarean section rate is only 10 to 15 percent, and the instrument delivery rate (forceps or vacuum) is no more than 5 percent. You also know a midwife will be caring for you during your labor and delivery. An obstetrician will not be far away should complications arise. Continuous electronic fetal monitoring is unusual as are episiotomies for delivery. (See chapter 6.) During labor, you are free to move about the labor and delivery area, take a relaxing jacuzzi bath, walk, or rock in a rocking chair.

Because relaxation techniques are being used and the midwife is constantly present to provide support, the need for epidural anesthesia is quite infrequent.

If your baby is in the breech position, i.e., buttocks first, vaginal delivery is frequently expected even if external version (turning the baby) is not successful. (See chapter 10.)

For most women who have had previous cesarean sections, a vaginal birth is planned also, and 70 to 80 percent of these women deliver normally. (See chapter 6.) This type of obstetric care system is neither fantasy nor impractical. In fact, in some medical facilities in the United States and Europe, this kind of care is already given today.

It <u>will</u> be the standard of care in the future if you and other American women apply pressure on your doctors, hospitals, insurance companies, and legislators to achieve these goals.

As a result of this system of care, there will be a natural reduction in malpractice suits and medical costs. More pregnant women will seek early and continued prenatal care, and the incidence of medical problems with newborn babies will remain very low.

But even more significant than these great benefits is the fact that you and other healthy pregnant women will have an opportunity to be in control of much of your own medical care during your pregnancies.

In order to achieve these very realistic, natural goals, the following changes are needed:

- A massive increase in the number and use of certified nurse midwives.
- Major changes in malpractice laws to reduce malpractice premiums and associated problems.
- An educated and assertive community of women who individually and collectively demand better from their medical care system.

The value of self-empowerment cannot be underestimated. The following true story, while quite dramatic and exceptional, clearly proves the point.

From the Doctor's Files

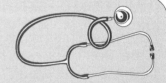

Se Vue came into my life on a very cold Saturday in January. Being Hmong, she had lived all of her 25 years in Southeast Asia and only four months before, she had left a refugee camp in Thailand and immigrated to the United States. Because her husband had relatives in Wisconsin, they settled here. When she first arrived, she had no coat, for such apparel isn't needed in the jungle climates of Laos and Thailand.

But the cold weather was not the only strange feature of her new home. She had no knowledge of most of the things we take for granted, such as reading, writing, cars, traffic, school systems, telephones, newspapers, American money, electrical appliances, and so on. Her people are mountain people, who were forced to flee at the end of the Vietnam War. Their ways are primitive and their beliefs, traditions, customs, manners, and value systems are totally different from any in the United States.

On that cold Saturday, Se Vue, through an interpreter, was asking me for help. She was pregnant for the sixth time and only about six weeks from her due date. All of her previous pregnancies had gone well and she had delivered normally five times. Three of those children had died of infections or malnutrition, or perhaps a combination of both. They believed that when a child dies, it is reincarnated into another, future child. This certainly helped them get through those deaths.

Se's immediate problem was another doctor and our legal system. She had been having a little vaginal bleeding, so her previous doctor had her get an ultrasound exam, which showed that her placenta was partly covering the cervix. In situations like this, a cesarean section is strongly recommended, because labor will lead to massive blood loss, which may seriously affect the baby or mother. The doctor had appropriately recommended that she have a cesarean section to avoid this dangerous situation.

She had no intention of having a cesarean. Her beliefs also included the concept that an incision in a person's body results in allowing one's good spirits to escape and bad spirits to enter. As a result, she would likely be a poor wife and mother and would be left alone by her husband and children in this cold and strange land.

As bizarre as this potential scenario sounded to me, it was very real to Se. The situation was made even more intense by the fact that her doctor was insistent on doing a cesarean for this baby's delivery. He was so insistent, in fact, that he was asking for a court order to require Se to undergo the cesarean for the sake of the life of the child.

Se never looked at my face during the time that she spoke, because that is considered to be very bad manners in her culture. Even though I could not understand a word she was saying, I could tell from her body language that she was very worried and upset. That morning, we looked at the baby and placenta with the ultrasound machine and verified that, indeed, the lowest portion of the placenta covered the

29

cervix. Se wanted to know if it was possible for her to deliver vaginally and live. My opinion was that she would need blood transfusions but, yes, she would live through it.

At that point, I asked her if she had any aversions to blood transfusions. Fortunately, she did not. In fact, someone else's good spirits could be helpful. (Sometimes, religious beliefs can be awfully confusing to the uninitiated.)

Then she asked if the baby would survive a vaginal delivery. I told her I wasn't sure. Maybe. I asked if a cesarean section would be acceptable to her if it appeared that the baby was in great jeopardy. Her answer was no. She wanted to know if I would agree to deliver her baby normally. I reluctantly agreed, only after I made it clear to her that this was very dangerous and could possibly result in death for both her and her child. We came to our mutually understood agreement, and then she asked me to testify in court so that she could avoid a court-ordered cesarean.

The case went to court the following Monday, and the judge was visibly relieved to avoid making the decision to force Se to have a cesarean section. This brave woman now had a doctor who would try his best to honor her requests, regardless of how dangerous they might be.

The next few weeks went by quietly, until Se went into labor on her own. She came into the Labor & Delivery area, bleeding profusely. We had previously arranged for several units of blood to be available, and within minutes of her arrival, she was getting some.

Her labor did not go quickly, and hours went by while she contracted and bled heavily. After her third unit of blood, her labor became more intense, which was encouraging. I began to develop concern over a problem in the fetal heart-rate tracing, although it was not yet life-threatening. At that time, I gave her another opportunity to change her mind about the cesarean, but she remained adamant in her opposition. Eventually, she began to push the baby down, and by that time, the fetal heart rhythm was really bothering me. I was definitely having "physician distress". We had transfused seven units of blood, given her other fluids, blood products, and oxygen. She finally delivered her baby, along with another large gush of blood and clots.

The baby required a few minutes of resuscitation, but eventually perked up and was doing quite nicely about six or seven minutes after delivery. Se herself did well, although she was fairly weak for a couple of days afterwards. She took some serious risks, not only for herself, but also for her baby. It was not what I had counseled her to do. It was very dangerous for her to deliver this way. However, because I was willing to bend a great deal in order to respect her autonomy, she was able to achieve her goal of avoiding an operation.

She returned six weeks later for her routine postpartum visit. She and her baby were doing very well. With her husband and an interpreter in the room, she surprised me by looking straight into my eyes and said, "Please forgive me for looking at your face while I speak to you. I have learned that American women can do this when they talk to their doctors. I hope I do not offend you." She continued, "I want you to know that I am very grateful to you for helping me. You have saved my life and all of my future lives also."

I often learn a lot about life from my patients. From Se, I learned how important respect for autonomy is in the doctor-patient relationship. I will remember her always.

Chapter 2
Midwives and Doctors

N ow that you realize <u>you</u> are in control of your pregnancy decisions, the first decision to make is the type of medical care you want for your pregnancy. Your pregnancy experience will be influenced greatly by the person you trust to care for you during this exciting time in your life.

This brings us to the next important thing to know: **For healthy women expecting an uncomplicated pregnancy, midwifery care is usually the better choice.**

If you have medical problems, which may complicate your pregnancy, or if you have had problems in previous pregnancies which concern you, your initial prenatal visit should be with a doctor.

Midwifery Care

Certified Nurse Midwives (CNMs) are registered nurses who have taken advanced training in the art and science of providing obstetric care. Certified midwives (CMs) enter the profession through an alternate pathway but are considered

33

to be equivalent to CNMs by the American College of Nurse-Midwives (ACNM). They usually only take care of healthy women with uncomplicated pregnancies and often work closely with obstetricians in a group practice.

A midwife is likely to be physically present and supportive throughout much, if not all, of a woman's labor. This is very important because her presence reduces maternal anxiety and tension, which generally results in faster labors with less need for pain medication or epidural anesthesia.

From the Doctor's Files

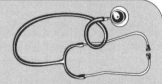

I have worked closely with Certified Nurse Midwives for more than 25 years and have learned a great deal from them.

The midwives in our clinic deliver about 35 percent of our babies. Their cesarean section rate hovers around 5 percent. This is dramatically lower than the national cesarean rate of 20-25 percent. Part of that low cesarean section rate is due to their low-risk patient population, but a major factor is their intense individualized attention to the laboring mothers.

There is an attitude among most midwives that most doctors do not share. It has to do with control. Midwives in general use more natural means to enhance the processes of labor and delivery than obstetricians do. **Obstetricians, in general, feel the need to be in charge, which leads to more inductions, epidural anesthesia, forceps deliveries, and cesarean sections.**

Besides certified nurse midwives and certified midwives, who are the best trained and most widely accepted, there are also "lay midwives" whose medical knowledge is limited.

While many healthy babies have been delivered by lay midwives, the quality of care becomes progressively more risky with the lower levels of training.

We recommend that you choose a midwife who is hospital-based, or associated with an accredited birth center. These midwives are primarily CNMs.

The percentage of women getting midwifery care has doubled in the past 10 years, but even so, it is less than 10 percent. There are two basic reasons for this: There are not enough CNMs to go around, and they are seen as competition by many obstetricians, who frequently try very hard to keep them out of the medical care system.

As consumers in the medical care system, pregnant women should seek out the care of midwives, encourage their doctors to bring CNMs into their community, and put pressure on their clinics and hospitals to incorporate the services of CNMs.

For information about CNMs in your area, or how best to encourage midwifery care, you can contact the American College of Nurse Midwives (ACNM) through their website, www.midwife.org or call them at 1-888-MIDWIFE.

Labor and Delivery Nurses

If you are unable to get a midwife to care for you, a person who can be extremely helpful and supportive during childbirth is your labor and delivery nurse.

Because these nurses often have years of experience caring for couples during labor and delivery, their skill level is very high, making them specialists in obstetric care. You might arrange to meet some of them during a prenatal or Lamaze class, or during a tour of the labor and delivery area prior to your due date. Nearly all hospitals welcome couples to take these tours.

Doulas

Individualized and personal attention, especially when you are in labor, can be extremely helpful. It has been shown that the continuous presence of a female birth assistant during labor may reduce the need for pain medication, the length of labor, and the likelihood of needing either a forceps or cesarean delivery.

Some men can provide the same help, but certainly not all. Some midwives or labor and delivery nurses can be there with you all the time, but they may have other laboring patients or responsibilities which may limit their time with you.

The common term for women who provide this service is "doula". Doulas are specially trained women who are present throughout labor and delivery, providing various physical comfort measures and emotional support for their clients.

If you are planning a hospital delivery and doulas are available in your community, your doctor or midwife can direct you to them. There may be a charge for her services, which will probably not be covered by insurance. You will need to ask her about this. You can find out more about doulas by calling Doulas of North America at 1-206-324-5440, or by checking their website at www.dona.com.

Birth Centers

Aside from hospitals, there are other medical facilities, called birth centers, which provide a safe environment for childbirth. In birth centers, women with low-risk pregnancies can labor and deliver with more personal freedoms than most hospitals provide, including freedom of movement, eating and drinking, showers, baths, and choices of delivery positions. The number of family and friends available for support is unlimited, and the mother and her baby are together throughout her postpartum stay.

All accredited birth centers must meet certain safety criteria, which stipulate conditions for quick transfer to a nearby hospital should complications arise.

As of July, 2001, the National Association of Childbearing Centers (NACC) has listed 70 certified birth centers in the United States, 42 of which are accredited by the Commission for the Accreditation of Birth Centers. Twenty-one states have no birth centers at all. For information about birth centers in your area, you can contact the NACC on its website at www.birthcenters.org.

Home Delivery

Lay midwives may offer home birth services. This practice is not generally recommended, but for women who are culturally or emotionally committed to home delivery, it can be a very satisfying experience. Unfortunately, home deliveries carry extreme health risks which are far less likely with a hospital delivery.

Interviewing a Midwife

If you are considering having a midwife care for you during your pregnancy, you should ask her certain questions at your first visit.

- Are you certified by the ACNM?
- Do you have a hospital-based practice?
- Will there be an obstetrician available at the time of delivery in case a problem arises?
- Will my insurance policy cover this midwifery care?
- Will you or one of the other midwives you work with definitely be there for me when I am in labor?
- Will I have all pain relief options available to me?

Doctors

Last year, of the four million American women having babies, all but 300,000 went to see doctors for their care. The vast majority of these doctors are obstetricians.

Obstetricians are physicians trained in the unique medical problems of women, especially in pregnancy. All are capable of doing cesarean sections, forceps or vacuum deliveries, and diagnosing and treating a wide variety of pregnancy-related medical problems.

Family practice physicians are medical doctors who specialize in the medical care of the entire family, including pregnant women. Nationally, about one-third of these doctors care for pregnant women. They usually take care of healthy women with uncomplicated pregnancies, and refer women with significant problems to obstetricians. Most do not perform cesareans or forceps deliveries.

Information about family physicians can be found at the website of the American Academy of Family Physicians (AAFP), www.aafp.org.

Nearly all doctors who take care of pregnant women do so in hospitals. There are still a few who do home deliveries, but they are rare.

Selecting a physician can sometimes be challenging. If you don't have a doctor you know and trust, you can often get good recommendations from friends or family members who have recently had babies. Other good sources of information are nurses, receptionists or other people who work in medical settings. Good and bad reputations of doctors are widely known in their institutions by their co-workers.

Sometimes it helps to make appointments with more than one doctor early in your pregnancy, and discuss your concerns with them. You will get an impression from this conversation, which will probably be an accurate barometer of how the two of you will be able to relate for the rest of your pregnancy.

The most important reason to see a doctor for your pregnancy care is safety. Physician-directed obstetric care, in spite of its occasional annoying interventions and unnecessary cesareans, is very safe for mothers and babies.

Today's healthy, pregnant American woman has every reason to feel confident that the medical care she receives will result in her remaining healthy after her baby is born. She also can expect, with 99 percent assurance, that her baby will survive. Throughout all of human history, until the last 20 or 30 years, this has not been so.

This wonderful news is due, in great part, to a century of tremendous improvements in public health planning and medical care.

If you decide later in your pregnancy that you want to switch your care to another doctor within the same health care system, it is easier than you may think. All you have to do is schedule an appointment with your new doctor and ask his receptionist or nurse to request that a copy of your medical records be transferred from your previous doctor's office. Don't feel bad. It happens all the time, for a wide variety of reasons.

Switching to a totally different health care system may be more of a problem, especially if your medical insurance restricts your choices. Check with your insurance provider. Many will cover only 80 percent of the charges if you switch out of the preferred medical system.

Paying 20 percent of your total obstetric bill to switch physicians may be too steep, but sometimes it seems like a bargain if you get the care you really believe is best. You have options in these circumstances, but they may cost you one to two thousand dollars, or more.

For more information about obstetric services in your area, as well as a great deal of pregnancy-related information, The American College of Obstetricians & Gynecologists (ACOG) can be contacted through their website, www.ACOG.org.

However, when choosing a doctor, you need to be aware of one of the problems doctors have; malpractice anxiety.

Malpractice Anxiety

About 75 percent of all obstetricians now practicing in the United States have been sued for malpractice. It is extremely stressful for those who are sued, and, as a result, they suffer a type of post-traumatic stress disorder, which may cause them to look at their patients as adversaries instead of allies during their pregnancies.

Your obstetrician's fear of malpractice suits is very real and may affect nearly every aspect of your care during pregnancy.

Even though obstetricians actually win the vast majority of cases that go to trial, the whole experience is a disaster, especially on a personal level. As a result, pregnant women bear the brunt of the pervasive fear that obstetricians have of being sued.

Unnecessary Cesarean Sections

The cesarean section rate in the United States in the 1990s has hovered around 22 to 24 percent. It was about 8 percent in the 1970s. What this means to you, is that you have nearly one chance in four of having a major abdominal operation to have a baby. That rate should be more like one in ten. **The main reason why pregnant women get unnecessary cesarean sections in this country is that their doctors are afraid of malpractice suits.** If, somehow, the fear of malpractice suits could be removed, the cesarean rate would plummet. Unfortunately, there is no such magic on the horizon.

Cesarean sections and recovery from them generally go well. (See chapter 5). The risks are relatively low, compared to other major operations. However, compared to vaginal deliveries, cesareans are 10 times more likely to cause major complications, cause far more recovery pain and other difficulties in the first several days after delivery, and result in vastly greater expense for medical care.

> The current rate of cesarean sections is a national medical disgrace.

"Physician Distress"

A common reason for unnecessary cesareans due to fear of malpractice suits is something called "fetal distress." It is a very poor term, which has no clear definition. Actually, the majority of the time, it should be called "physician distress", or sometimes even "nurse distress."

"Fetal distress" refers to a worrisome fetal heart rate tracing during labor, which may indicate that the baby has developed a severe problem due to a lack of oxygen. The worry is that if not enough oxygen gets to the baby during labor, he may become neurologically damaged, develop cerebral palsy, or even die. In reality, this situation occurs only once or twice in every thousand deliveries, but the fear of its occurrence is so great that over-reading of fetal heart-rate monitoring strips occurs rather frequently. As a result, many babies are born by emergency cesarean who otherwise would have been just fine if allowed to be delivered vaginally. The driving force behind most cesareans which result from fetal distress is fear, and a big part of that is the fear of being sued for malpractice.

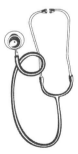

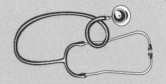

From the Doctor's Files

All this fear about fetal distress and malpractice suits has led obstetricians to do a lot of annoying, aggravating, and sometimes, though rarely, dangerous things to pregnant women in labor. We have fooled ourselves into thinking we are doing these things for you and not to you. In fact, the majority of the time, procedures such as fetal scalp sampling, fetal scalp electrodes, and even continuous fetal monitoring itself, are for us, so that we can feel reassured that if the baby does eventually develop cerebral palsy in several months, that we will not lose a malpractice suit. We are trapped by the system into doing these things, and you may be trapped into having them done to you.

How Lawyers Affect Your Obstetric Care

There are a lot of things your doctor may do during your pregnancy that have nothing whatsoever to do with quality care, and have everything to do with misguided plans to reduce concerns about being sued.

Doctors, in general, know no more about law than lawyers know about medicine. When faced with legal concerns, they generally take the legal advice and follow instructions. Lawyers insist that you sign consent forms. Lawyers insist on documentation of every possible detail when you are in labor, thus, the fetal heart-rate monitor. Lawyers counsel medical facilities to do whatever possible to avoid an expensive and painful lawsuit. However, when doctors follow legal advice too well, they can end up destroying one of their most valuable assets: the ability to develop a trusting relationship with their patients.

Malpractice attorneys who represent unhappy patients are also a big part of the problem. The potential for huge amounts of money in medical malpractice cases often leads to rather marginal suits in hopes of a big settlement. These lawyers get one-third of all the "winnings," but get nothing if they lose.

If you call your doctor's office and say, "I have a bad cold and I'm 20 weeks pregnant. What can I take that is safe?" many nurses, upon instructions from their doctors, will tell you to take nothing more than acetaminophen. The truth is, at that point in your pregnancy, you can safely take almost any over-the-counter remedy that you can find for relief of your symptoms. (See chapter 3.) Your doctor most likely knows this, but because of his fear of getting sued, you will be told what he wants you to hear.

When you get an ultrasound done, does the technologist spend time showing the baby to you and your husband or significant other? Are you allowed to bring a videotape so that you can tape the ultrasound exam and keep it forever? No? Well, the only reason you aren't allowed these perfectly appropriate activities is fear of malpractice on the part of either the radiologist in charge, or your doctor.

Our clinic does ultrasound exams on 98 percent of the pregnant women who come to us. All of them are encouraged to bring whomever would like to see the baby, along with a blank videotape, when they have their scan done. We tape the event for them, and they take the tapes home. This is nearly always an exciting and fun experience for the new parents, and we want them to enjoy it. We have done this now for well over 30,000 pregnancies without any lawsuits. The positive experiences we have had with parents are well worth any potential malpractice concerns.

If you have an ultrasound done, you have every right to expect to be shown your baby in detail and should demand the opportunity to videotape the scan. If you are not allowed to do this, you know that your doctor is more interested in his misguided fears than he is in your happiness. This would be a good thing to discuss with him.

Does your doctor or his nurse insist that you sign some kind of consent form for ultrasounds, amniocenteses, routine pre-natal care, normal vaginal delivery, etc.? These forms, in truth, have almost no real legal power in the case of a mal-practice suit, but some lawyer has convinced your doctor that it is a wise thing to do. It is not. It is just another barrier in the way of developing a trusting relationship with your doctor. If you are in this situation, you should tell him that you feel that signing the consent form is an intrusion on the doctor-patient relationship, and that you resent it. Perhaps if enough patients tell him this, he will get the message.

Unfortunately, the fear of malpractice suits is a fact of life which all physicians have to deal with in their own ways. Keep this in mind as you go through your pregnancy.

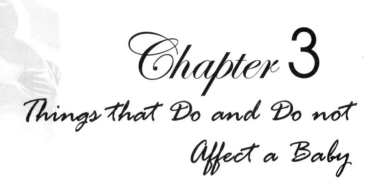

Chapter 3
Things that Do and Do not Affect a Baby

A fter the initial excitement of finding out that you are, indeed, pregnant, the next feeling you should expect is one of being protective. You will want your baby to grow and develop in a safe environment within you. Therefore, you will seek information on how best to do that.

Unfortunately, much of what you are told about pregnancy care is untrue and often leads to unnecessary anxiety and suffering.

Some of the information you get when you talk to your friends, your doctor, or your midwife may be old or incorrect, and the prenatal books and internet sources on the subject are frequently contradictory. The information in this chapter should clarify a great deal of that misinformation.

Emotional Stress

We are often asked about the effect of emotional stress on the developing baby. It is a difficult question to answer, because people respond in many different ways to stress.

Some women handle the most difficult situations without so much as a flutter of anxiety, while others get in a panic over seemingly ordinary problems.

It is fair to say that most pregnant women who feel emotional stress have little to fear from the effects of that stress on their developing babies. However, if a woman becomes so stressed that it significantly affects her health, her diet, or her long-term emotional stability, it can cause serious problems.

These problems may be premature labor, poor fetal growth (due to poor nutrition, drugs, or smoking), or in the case of those who need anti-anxiety medications such as Valium, newborn drug-withdrawal problems.

Physical Stress

Most ordinary physical activity has no significant effect on fetal growth, development, or risk of premature delivery. Healthy pregnant women can usually continue to do the same athletic activities they are used to doing until they become too uncomfortable. Contact sports, however, should be stopped.

Exercise

If you are used to a particular activity, even athletics, you should be able to continue doing it well into your pregnancy. There are some restrictions, however, and your previous obstetric history is important. You need to discuss this with your doctor or midwife at your first prenatal visit.

As with all physical activity during pregnancy, you will find that you need to slow down as your baby gets bigger. This is particularly true for women used to strenuous activity, such as aerobic exercising.

During pregnancy, there are many physiological changes which will directly affect your cardiac output and pulse rate. Your heart works harder, pushing more blood into the circulation with every beat. This means that when your pulse increases to, say, 120 beats per minute during pregnancy, it is doing far more work than at the same heart rate outside of pregnancy.

Therefore, when doing exercises, you should not push yourself until you reach the same pulse that you did previously. A maximum heart rate of 120 to 130 beats per minute is appropriate for aerobic exercising.

Physical Trauma

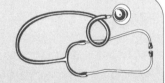

From the Doctor's Files

One summer day, I was called to see a woman who was being admitted to the Intensive Care Unit. She was 24 weeks pregnant, and her car had just been run over by a train. She had been sitting in the middle of the front seat. The man on her left was driving, and he was killed. The man on her right was also killed.

She was barely alive when she got to the Emergency Ward and was quickly taken to the operating room where, among other things, her fractured pelvis and thigh bone were repaired and her hemorrhaging spleen was removed. Her head injury also needed surgery.

When I first saw her, she was unconscious and literally bandaged from head to toe. My job was to evaluate the status of her pregnancy, and more specifically, to identify by ultrasound any traumatic injury to the baby. I looked carefully and could identify no injury. The baby was just fine, and I'm happy to say, delivered about three months later without any apparent problems.

The point of this true story is to demonstrate that inside his mother's uterus, surrounded by amniotic fluid, a baby is in a very safe place. It usually takes a great deal of blunt trauma to injure a baby.

Occasionally, however, automobile accidents, or punches and kicks to the stomach can lead to preterm labor or placental separation and bleeding.

Lesser trauma, such as slipping on the ice or having your three-year-old bouncing on your pregnant uterus rarely leads to serious difficulty.

Sharp trauma with knives, bullets, or flying glass, for example, is much less common but potentially much more serious.

Work

Most working pregnant women and their babies do very well, and most women will be able to continue working until very late in their pregnancies. However, if your job requires long hours of standing or lifting, you have an increased risk of delivering early. It is a good idea to discuss this with your doctor, especially if you have had a previous premature delivery.

Work Restrictions for Pregnant Women
- Limiting repetitive stooping and bending to less than 10 times per hour.
- Limiting repetitive climbing of ladders to less than three times per eight-hour shift.
- Limiting repetitive lifting to less than 50 pounds at 20 weeks gestation, intermittent heavy lifting at 30 weeks gestation, and standing to less than 30 minutes per hour at 32 weeks gestation.

With these exceptions, employment may be continued to term. Further details of guidelines can be obtained from the American College of Obstetrics and Gynecology on the internet at www.acog.org.

Hot Tubs, Saunas, and Whirlpools

Before your 11th week of pregnancy, there may be a very small, perhaps only theoretical, chance that an increase in your body temperature (over 102°F) may result in a spinal defect in your baby. After these weeks, there is no known problem with hot tubs, saunas, or whirlpools. Therefore, you should try to avoid hot tubs, saunas, and whirlpools in the first three months of your pregnancy. You may relax and enjoy them any time thereafter.

From the Nurse's Notes

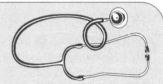

Some pregnant women we have seen have carried their unnecessary concern on this matter to extremes. One woman did not take a bath or a shower throughout her entire pregnancy because she was worried that she might do something awful to her baby. She stayed clean by using cold sponge baths. This kind of overreaction is not unexpected, given the inappropriate information pregnant women often read in newspapers and magazines.

Electric Blankets

There is no good scientific evidence that miscarriages can be caused by electric blankets. The potential for problems exists only if the body temperature goes above 102°F in the first 11 weeks. No human being would willingly stay in that kind of heat, especially not a pregnant one. Therefore, you have little to fear from electric blankets.

Lying on Your Back

Some pregnant women have a problem lying on their back for more than a few minutes. They feel nauseated, weak, and hot. This is due to a marked, temporary decrease in blood pressure caused by the pregnant uterus compressing the large vein that carries most of the blood from the lower half of the body back to the heart. We see this commonly in the ultrasound room. Simply turning to either side completely resolves the problem within seconds. This temporary light-headedness is of no importance to the developing baby.

If you are lying on your back at home and begin to feel uncomfortable, you will naturally turn to your side and feel better. This occurs spontaneously, even when you are sleeping. **Therefore, you can sleep in whatever position feels most comfortable.**

Raising Your Arms Above Your Head

We have included this because a surprising number of pregnant women have heard that raising your arms above your head during pregnancy causes the cord to loop around the baby's neck or get tied in knots. This is simply not true. As a side note, about 20 percent of babies are born with at least one loop of cord around their necks. It rarely causes any harm.

Cats and Kitty Litter

There is a disease called Toxoplasmosis that may seriously affect a developing fetus. It rarely does so in the United

States, but does so more often in other countries where eating habits are different. The disease is spread by a protozoan (a one-celled organism) found most commonly in raw meat and on the ground from animal droppings.

American women rarely eat raw meat, but their cats might, especially if they are allowed to roam and hunt outside. If a cat eats an infected rodent, he will soon pass tiny toxoplasma eggs in his stool. If he uses the litter box to deposit this stool, the person who cleans this box has a chance of becoming infected as well. If that person is pregnant, the developing baby may become infected also, with potentially disastrous results. Cats who live inside and eat only prepared cat food will rarely, if ever, get or transmit toxoplasmosis.

Therefore, you can take care of your cat's litter the same as you did before your pregnancy if you have an exclusively housebound cat. But, if your cat is a hunter outside, you have a choice of safe things to do:

- Have someone else clean the litter box.
- Wear a surgical mask and do it yourself, being sure to wash your hands afterwards.
- Get a blood test early in pregnancy to check your immunity to Toxoplasmosis and act accordingly.
- Have your cat tested by a veterinarian.

Additionally, always wash vegetables and fruit well before eating them, stay away from raw or undercooked meat, wash your hands thoroughly after handling raw meat, and use gloves when working in the garden.

Getting a Perm

There are a variety of chemicals you are exposed to whenever you get a permanent. Fortunately, only a tiny amount gets absorbed through your scalp, and there is no evidence whatsoever that getting a new hairstyle will in any way affect your pregnancy or baby.

That may not be true for the person who does the perm. There is reason to believe that frequent skin exposure to those chemicals over a long period of time may increase the risk of having a miscarriage. No other pregnancy-related problems are to be expected. Wearing gloves will reduce this risk.

Therefore, you can ignore your Aunt Sally's advice and get a perm, or two, or three during your pregnancy. Pregnancy is a time when you may feel that you are not very attractive and the psychological lift of a new hairstyle can be very helpful. If you work in a beauty shop and frequently have your hands in chemicals, you should wear gloves consistently. This information is true for hair dyes as well.

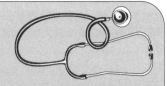

From the Doctor's Files

I was seeing a pregnant woman in her mid 30s who began showing up for her prenatal visits wearing scarves or hats to cover her hair. One day she took off her hat to lie down on the exam table, and I noticed that her naturally gray roots were about an inch long, giving her hair an interesting two-toned look.

I do not usually comment on a patient's appearance, but it was obvious that she needed a little help. I gently mentioned the safety involved in getting hair dyed during pregnancy. She came back two weeks later with dark roots, a smile, and no hat.

Diet Soft Drinks

Aspartame (Nutrasweet) is probably the most extensively studied food additive ever approved by the FDA. Therefore, you can feel very comfortable knowing that ingestion of aspartame-sweetened products during pregnancy or breastfeeding does not represent a significant risk to developing babies.

Saccharine is also an artificial sweetener, but it is used far less often than aspartame in diet foods and drinks. It does not cause babies to develop abnormalities nor any other known problems as they grow up. There is no <u>human</u> evidence that an increased risk of cancer occurs, although there is such a risk for certain laboratory animals.

Therefore, you can continue to drink diet soft drinks if you wish. Keep in mind though that many soft drinks (with or without aspartame) contain a fair amount of sodium, which may cause you to retain fluids or increase your blood pressure. For most pregnant women, this is not a problem, but if you have increased blood pressure or swelling in the last trimester, cutting down on soft drink consumption may be helpful.

During pregnancy, you need to drink huge amounts of fluids just to keep up with the natural needs of your body. Because many women have been told to stay away from diet drinks, they drink large amounts of sodas, juices, lemonades, etc., all containing a generous amount of sugar. This not only results in rapid and excessive weight gain in pregnancy, but may also lead to unnecessarily large babies who are more difficult to deliver.

For years, pregnant women have been told by doctors and nurses to stay away from diet drinks. This is a mistake. If you are otherwise going to drink large volumes of fluids with sugar in them, it would be better for you to drink diet drinks with aspartame in them instead. Better yet, drink water.

Eating for Two

Adequate, balanced nutrition in pregnancy is very important. There are many good information sources which cover appropriate diet in pregnancy, so we won't repeat all that here. Pregnant women are frequently told they need to gain about 25 to 30 pounds in order to maximize their baby's chances for a healthy start in life. This is usually, but not always, accurate.

Your growing baby requires that you eat a balanced nutritional diet. If, when you started your pregnancy, you were about average weight, you will gain that 25 pounds or so. However, if you are heavy and eat appropriately during your pregnancy, you may only gain 10 to 15 pounds. There is nothing wrong with that.

The growing baby is not really affected by exactly how many pounds you gain, but more by the nutrition you take in. If you eat properly and don't focus on the exact number of pounds you gain, you and your baby will do just fine.

Caffeine

Caffeine is a drug. It is found in varying amounts in coffee, non-herbal teas, soft drinks, some pain medicines, and even a variety of foods. Heavy daily intake of caffeine (approximately five cups of caffeinated coffee, 10 soft drinks, or 10 cups of tea) is associated with an increased risk of a variety of pregnancy-related problems, especially miscarriages, infertility, and withdrawal symptoms for newborn babies.

A moderate daily amount of caffeine (about two to three cups of coffee, or four to five soft drinks or cups of tea) is not associated with fetal abnormalities, miscarriages, preterm delivery, or poor fetal growth. Because caffeine content in different drinks varies significantly, it is difficult, if not impossible, to be more exact.

Therefore, you may drink moderate amounts of caffeinated beverages in pregnancy. You should also be aware that high daily doses of caffeine taken while breastfeeding may result in irritable babies.

Alcohol

Alcohol is a dangerous drug outside of pregnancy, and even more so during pregnancy. If taken in significant amounts throughout pregnancy, it may cause your baby to have facial abnormalities, defects of the central nervous system, mild to moderate mental retardation and poor growth.

This is a problem called Fetal Alcohol Syndrome. It is something no mother wants for her child. Significant alcohol use late in pregnancy may lead to future behavioral and developmental problems.

The question about alcohol and pregnancy is, how much alcohol is safe to drink when pregnant? The easy (and incorrect) answer usually told to pregnant women is none.

In looking at all the statistics and data of the studies done on alcohol and pregnancy, it is clear that if a pregnant woman consumes less than two drinks per week, there is no evidence that her baby will be negatively affected.

In general, completely avoiding alcohol is the best policy. Having two drinks may lead to three, then four, etc. But an occasional glass of wine with dinner will not cause any harm.

Smoking

Smoking cigarettes is associated with a variety of bad pregnancy outcomes, including miscarriage, preterm delivery, and poor fetal growth. Even as few as one to five cigarettes a day is associated with a higher risk of small babies. It does not cause physical deformities.

Perhaps just as important, but seldom mentioned, is the effect of secondhand smoke. Babies in an environment of smokers have far more troubles with upper respiratory infections, nasal congestion and ear infections. What that means for the mother is a lot of sleepless nights that could have been avoided by keeping the home smoke-free. There is also good evidence that infants exposed to cigarette smoke have two to eight times the risk of dying of Sudden Infant Death Syndrome (SIDS) compared to those infants whose parents do not smoke.

You should stop smoking if you are pregnant. If you have been a heavy smoker and can't seem to quit, reducing the number of cigarettes to fewer than five per day will help. Ask your doctor about smoking intervention programs.

Cocaine

Of all the "recreational" drugs available, cocaine is the most dangerous to a developing baby. Its use frequently causes a wide variety of very significant newborn problems, such as premature birth, strokes, poor growth, congenital defects, and neuropsychological damage and death. Because it also may cause placental separation, called abruption, which usually results in hemorrhage, cocaine can lead to maternal death as well. **Cocaine and pregnancy are a very bad combination.**

On a related subject, phenylcyclidine (PCP) has also been shown to be very harmful to the developing fetal brain. Common features of newborns whose mothers took PCP include irritability, jitteriness, and poor feeding. Some of these problems may be permanent.

Household Pesticides

There are many different chemicals that may be used as pesticides. Agricultural pesticides may not be the same stuff that your local pest control service spreads around the house. Five active ingredients in older pesticides—

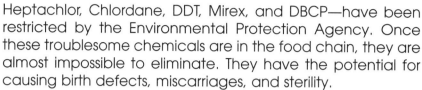

Heptachlor, Chlordane, DDT, Mirex, and DBCP—have been restricted by the Environmental Protection Agency. Once these troublesome chemicals are in the food chain, they are almost impossible to eliminate. They have the potential for causing birth defects, miscarriages, and sterility.

Fortunately, household pesticides generally do not contain non-degradable, dangerous chemicals. The pesticides we use around the house are surprisingly safe for humans because they oxidize or break down very quickly (in about one to two hours) and, therefore, pose little risk for pregnant women or their babies. The chemicals used as typical yard or home pesticides have not been shown to lead to birth defects or behavioral problems. However, some people have annoying allergic reactions to them, resulting in skin rashes or even mild asthmatic attacks.

A word of caution is needed here. There are over 100,000 different chemicals that may be found in varying concentrations in the United States. Very few have been adequately tested as far as their potential toxicity to developing babies. The effects of combinations of these chemicals are mostly unknown. Because of the lack of knowledge about these chemicals, you should protect yourself and avoid unnecessary exposure to potentially toxic chemicals.

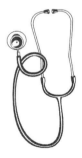

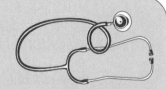

From the Doctor's Files

One day, I was listening to a talk show on National Public Radio. The subject was the risk of environmental chemicals in pregnancy, and they invited telephone calls from listeners. One woman called because she had her house sprayed with pesticides on the very day she had found out that she was pregnant. She was extremely early in the pregnancy at the time. She said that her doctor told her not to worry, but she worried anyway. Now, two and a half years later, she asked the expert on the radio show when she would start seeing behavioral and neurological problems in her two-year-old son. He seemed normal so far, but she was still waiting for problems to appear. The expert told her, appropriately, that she should not expect any problems to appear and to stop worrying. He said it much nicer and gentler than that, but that was the gist of his answer.

I felt very sorry for the caller. She had it in her mind that her child was irretrievably damaged, and she was just waiting for evidence of deterioration. How sad. How maddening that she would feel the need to act this way because someone, somewhere, had convinced her of something that was not true. In her case, ignorance was not bliss. It was torture.

Painting

Years ago, paints often contained unacceptable levels of arsenic or lead, which have the potential to cause a wide variety of serious health problems, including birth defects. More recently, concern has been raised about the levels of mercury in paint. However, the possibility of your absorbing any of these dangerous elements while painting a room is almost zero, and thus the likelihood of absorbing enough to cause birth defects is very low. There is also no evidence that the solvent you absorb while painting that room has any effect on a developing baby. Breathing paint fumes can make a person nauseated or lightheaded. This is especially so in pregnancy, when these feelings are common anyway. Using a mask, having a fan going in the room, or opening a window while painting can reduce these symptoms.

Sometimes, paint jobs require stripping of the old paint. This may best be a job for someone who is not pregnant. Some old paints contain lead, which is a potent health hazard, especially for your baby's developing brain cells.

Painting a room is very different from working in a factory that makes paint and associated solvents. The exposure to potentially dangerous chemicals in these factories is markedly increased, and a pregnant woman should consider leaving any such environment for the duration of her pregnancy.

Noise

No one knows for sure how loud or constant noise has to be to have the potential for causing fetal hearing problems. We know that fetuses hear very well, and that amniotic fluid transmits sound nicely. If the noise is too loud for you, it is probably too loud for your baby. If you are pregnant and work in a setting that is so loud that you need to wear protection for your ears, your baby may have the potential for suffering hearing problems.

Computers, Monitors, and Microwave Ovens

There has been a great deal of testing on potential hazards of these machines, and no deleterious effects have been found for developing fetuses.

Medicines in Pregnancy

You will have to make choices during your pregnancy about taking medicines or getting diagnostic x-ray tests done. You should make wise decisions based on facts, not fear. Let us look at some facts.

For today's pregnant woman, 1979 is a year that will live in infamy. In a court of law in Orlando, Florida, scientific knowledge and common sense were ignored, and legal maneuvers and pity were used to win a lawsuit against the manufacturers of a medicine called Bendectin.

Until then, millions of pregnant women had taken Bendectin, a combination of an antihistamine and a vitamin, for relief of nausea in early pregnancy. It was a very popular drug because it worked very well. At its peak usage, nearly one in every four pregnant women took Bendectin for relief of morning sickness. Because it was used in early pregnancy by huge numbers of women, it was relatively easy to study its potential effects on developing babies.

It is nearly impossible to scientifically prove the absolute safety of a drug, but studies on Bendectin came as close as possible to that goal. Nonetheless, the parents of a baby born with disfigured arms sued the Merrill Pharmaceutical Company, claiming that the Bendectin she had taken in early pregnancy had caused the baby's defects. The jury, swayed by the sight of the child's heart-wrenching disabilities and the pleas of the parents' attorney, gave the verdict to the parents in spite of all scientific evidence to the contrary.

The jury may also have been influenced by public hysteria on the subject, fueled in part by outrageous stories such as this one in the <u>National Enquirer</u> that year:

"Experts Reveal...Common Drug Causing Deformed Babies--In a monstrous scandal that could be far larger than the thalidomide horror, untold thousands of babies are being born with hideous defects after their mothers took an anti-nausea drug (Bendectin) during early pregnancy."

The judgement of this trial has had far-reaching effects for pregnant women. First, Bendectin was taken off the market by the Merrill Company because of the astronomical costs of defending any further suits against them over its use. As a result, millions of pregnant women were denied the opportunity to get medical relief from the terribly annoying problem of morning sickness.

Secondly, doctors and pharmaceutical companies became paranoid about giving pregnant women <u>any</u> medication for fear of being sued if a baby was born with an abnormality. As a result, millions of pregnant women have suffered from a variety of other treatable problems because they were told to avoid taking any medicine.

Thirdly, an irrational subculture has evolved, which warns women against using any medicine in pregnancy, but encourages the use of teas, herbs, minerals, etc. for a variety of common pregnancy maladies. As a result, instead of using a variety of medicines tested and known to be safe, millions of pregnant women are using totally natural but untested materials, whose potency and safety in pregnancy is completely unknown.

There is no doubt that certain medicines have the potential to cause developmental changes to occur in babies, resulting in horrible disfigurements of varying kinds. Fortunately, these situations are rare. It may surprise you to know that most prescription medicines, if taken for a short time in pregnancy, are harmless to the developing baby.

The time during pregnancy when medicines, chemicals, herbs, or teas may have the most effect on the baby is between four weeks and twelve weeks after the last menstrual period (or two to ten weeks after conception). This is the time when your baby's organs are being formed.

You will be faced with choices throughout your pregnancy. One of those choices is whether to take a medicine during an illness or to suffer without it. There are other potential concerns, usually less severe, and these need to be known as well. Listed below are a variety of common over-the-counter medicines and potential pregnancy-related concerns about them.

Analgesics

There are two basic types of over-the-counter (OTC) medications used to relieve general pain: acetaminophen and non-steroidal anti-inflammatory drugs (NSAIDs). NSAIDs include aspirin, Ibuprofen, and Naproxyn.

Acetaminophen, better known by such brand names as Tylenol, Tempra, Excedrin, and Vanquish, is the one analgesic doctors can comfortably recommend during pregnancy because of its proven safety. It is helpful for minor headaches and other minor pains.

Aspirin, found in Anacin, Bufferin, Bayer, and Ascriptin, has not been shown to cause fetal malformations. However, used in the last two months of pregnancy, it may cause temporary maternal or newborn bleeding problems. Long-term use is associated with prolonged pregnancy and labor problems. Aspirin is not better than acetaminophen for pain relief. Low-dose aspirin may be useful in those rare cases of women with clotting disorders which lead to stillborn or under-grown babies. There is no known harm in using one baby aspirin a day for this problem.

Ibuprofen, found in such medications as Advil, Motrin, and Nuprin, seems to give better pain relief for the headaches and low backaches pregnant women often have. **However, the use of Ibuprofen after 32 weeks is not suggested for a variety**

of reasons: Bleeding disorders, problems with fetal urine production and pulmonary circulation, as well as prolonged pregnancy. The same is true for naproxen, found in Aleve and Naprosyn. Ibuprofen has not been shown to cause fetal malformations.

From the Doctor's File

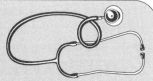

When my patients ask me what they should take for pain relief during pregnancy, I first talk to them about non-medical relief methods, such as heat, massage or stress reduction, and work-related issues. If an analgesic is suggested, I usually suggest Ibuprofen (200 mg) taken sporadically if they are less than 32 weeks along and Acetaminophen sporadically after that.

Antacids

Most pregnant women suffer at least occasionally from heartburn. This is usually relieved temporarily by any number of different kinds of antacids. Most of these have either magnesium hydroxide plus aluminum hydroxide (found in Maalox, Mylanta, and Gaviscon) or calcium carbonate (found in TUMS, Rolaids, and Di-Gel) in them. Calcium carbonate seems to last longer and also supplies additional calcium and is therefore favored in pregnancy. None are known to cause fetal problems when taken according to the manufacturer's suggestions.

On occasion, heartburn is so bad that you need something stronger, such as Famotidine (Pepcid), Nizatidine (Zantac), or Ranitidine (Pepcid AC). These are considered safe during pregnancy, even by their manufacturers. Avoid Cimetidine (Tagamet) which may (theoretically, at least) have hormonal effects on the fetus.

Additionally, anti-flatulents containing Simethicone (found in Gas-Ex, Phazyme, and Anti-Gas) can be very helpful for bloating discomforts throughout pregnancy. There are no known fetal side effects from this medication. Be sure to take a dose of at least 80 mg after meals and especially at bedtime. Anything less may not be effective.

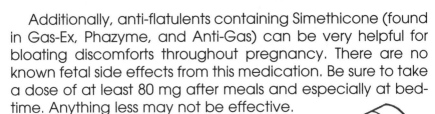

Antihistamines

Antihistamines have many possible uses: relief of allergy symptoms, relief of nausea in early pregnancy, sleep aid, and as an additive in many decongestants.

Diphenhydramine, Meclizine, Dimenhydrinate, and Chlorpheniramine are generic names for the most commonly used antihistamines. There is no evidence that they cause fetal malformations except in those rare instances when mothers have taken them shortly before a premature delivery, and an eye disorder called retrolental fibroplasia has developed. High doses late in pregnancy may lead to uterine contractions or withdrawal symptoms in a newborn.

Diphenhydramine (found in Benadryl, Unisom, and Tylenol PM) has been very helpful for relief of allergy symptoms and as a sleep aid.

Meclizine (found in Antivert, Bonine, and Dramamine II) used in conjunction with vitamin B6 occasionally works wonders for women with nausea and vomiting of early pregnancy.

Dimenhydrinate (found in Dramamine) is very helpful for motion sickness and as a sleep aid.

Chlorpheniramine (found in Nyquil, Dimetapp, Chlortrimeton, and Coricidin) is found in a variety of combination medications for relief of cold symptoms.

One antihistamine to avoid in pregnancy and breastfeeding is Clemastine (found in Tavist-D and Tavist-I). The American Academy of Pediatrics warns that its use may result in drowsy or irritable babies.

Cough Medications

Most pure over-the-counter cough medications contain either Dextromethorphan (DM) and/or Guaiafenesin, which we can recommend during pregnancy. There are no studies showing an increased risk of human malformations with these medications. Unfortunately, these are frequently combined with a variety of decongestants, antihistamines and analgesics, and the combinations are difficult to study scientifically. Be sure to check the ingredients carefully before taking these medications.

Decongestants

The dizzying array of decongestants and cold and cough preparations in your local drug store is enough to intimidate even the most conscientious and knowledgeable consumer. In an effort to consolidate this information into a usable format, just remember one word: Pseudoephedrine.

The safety of Pseudoephedrine in the first 13 weeks of pregnancy is uncertain. From then on, taken on occasion for symptoms of a cold, it should cause no pregnancy related problems. For those women who have high blood pressure problems, Pseudoephedrine may increase blood pressure and thus you should consult with your physician first.

Other decongestants contain either Phenylephrine, Phenylpropanolamine, Bromopheniramine, or Ephedrine and should be avoided during pregnancy. Before buying a decongestant, look at the list of ingredients carefully.

Stool Softeners and Laxatives

Natural fibers such as Psyllium (found in Metamucil and Perdiem) and Methylcellulose (found in Citracel) work as bulk producers rather than stimulants of the intestinal smooth muscle. They are safe throughout pregnancy when taken according to the instructions.

Stool softeners containing Docusate (found in Colace, Dialose, and Surfak) are also safe in pregnancy if taken according to instructions.

Laxatives should only be used if stool softeners and bulk agents are unsuccessful in relieving constipation. No specific pregnancy-related problems are known for laxatives, which contain Senna (found in Senekot), Magnesium Hydroxide (found in Phillip's Milk of Magnesia or Haley's MO), Casanthral (found in Pericolace and Doxidan), Bisacodyl (found in Dulcolax, Correctol, Feen-a-Mint), or Phenolphthalein (found in Ex-Lax). These last two are rather potent laxatives.

If you find you need to take laxatives more than three times in a week, you should discuss your problem with your doctor. Long-term use of colon-stimulating laxatives is potentially harmful. Laxatives do not initiate labor.

Antidiarrheals

Neither Kaolin/Pectin (found in Kaopectate, Donnagel, and Rheaban) nor Loperamide (found in Imodium AD and Pepto Diarrhea Control) are known to cause fetal or pregnancy-related problems. Bismuth subsalicylate (found in Pepto-Bismol) contains an aspirin-like chemical and should be avoided in pregnancy.

It is important to know that premature labor is sometimes associated with diarrhea. Intestinal cramps may, on occasion, be difficult to distinguish from uterine contractions. These medicines will not reduce uterine contractions. Thus, if you continue to suffer from cramping in spite of taking an antidiarrheal medicine, consider the possibility of uterine contractions as the cause of your discomfort.

Antifungal Agents

Antifungal agents are used for the relief of vaginal yeast infections, which are very common in pregnancy.

Miconazole, Butoconazole, Chlortrimazole are all very similar generic medications. You may find these in the drug store under the common brand names of Monistat, Femstat, Gyne-Lotrimin, or Mycelex. The use of these medications in pregnancy has not been associated with any fetal problems. However, symptoms of a yeast infection of the vagina may be confused with other infectious problems. Diabetes may lead to frequent yeast infections of the vagina. Therefore, if your symptoms persist in spite of treatment with this medication, or if the problem is recurrent, you should discuss this with your doctor.

Precautions

The potential fetal effects of either combination drugs (more than one medicine in one tablet or liquid) or a combination of different, separate medicines are completely unknown. **In general, you should avoid using combination drugs in the first 12 weeks of your pregnancy, when susceptibility to malformations is at its peak.**

Your reactions to medicines may vary depending on your particular circumstances. The information in this chapter is provided for educational purposes only. Consult your own physician regarding the applicability of any opinions or recommendations with respect to your symptoms or medical condition.

In addition to these over-the-counter medications, your doctor may prescribe a wide variety of other medicines for you. Be sure he knows what medications you are currently using, as there may be some potential for problems when combining medicines.

Vaccinations

The following vaccinations can be safely administered during pregnancy if necessary:

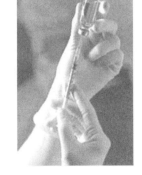

- Tetanus
- Diphtheria
- Hepatitis A&B
- Influenza
- Rabies
- Pneumonia
- Typhoid fever
- Inactive polio vaccine
of enhanced potency

The following vaccinations should be avoided in pregnancy if possible:

- MMR (measles, mumps, rubella)
- Varicella (chicken pox)
- Yellow fever
- Oral polio
- Lyme Disease
- Vaccinia (small pox)

Vitamins

Folic acid is a vitamin which, when taken in the months prior to pregnancy and also in the first three months, reduces the risk of a variety of fetal abnormalities. A dose of 400 micrograms per day is the recommended dose. Folic acid can be obtained without a prescription in nearly every drug store. It is a wise thing to take.

Most pregnant American women take prenatal multiple vitamins. However, for the majority of healthy women, the dietary intake of vitamins is easily sufficient to supply not only their needs, but the needs of their babies as well. Prenatal multiple vitamins commonly increase nausea in early pregnancy, cause constipation and bloating, and may cost in the range of $15 to $25 for 100 pills.

If you have a well-balanced diet and have been taking folic acid, taking prenatal vitamins routinely is unnecessary. They may actually cause more harm than good.

Calcium

Calcium is an essential mineral used to help build your baby's bones and eventually, his teeth. Pregnant women require about 1,000 milligrams per day. This requirement is easily met by drinking three cups of milk (non-fat is okay) per day. Other excellent sources of calcium are cheese, yogurt, fortified orange juice, sardines, dark green leafy vegetables (such as spinach, collard, kale & turnip greens), salmon with bones, nuts and seeds.

If you don't take in enough calcium during your pregnancy, your baby doesn't suffer because he will get enough from the calcium in your bones. However, you may suffer because of an increased risk of osteoporosis (fragile bones) later in life.

If you have a decent, well-balanced diet, neither you nor your baby will benefit from taking additional calcium tablets during your pregnancy.

Iron

Iron is used to make hemoglobin, which carries oxygen in red blood cells to all of the organs in your body. Your baby needs it and will take it from you. Therefore, pregnant women need more iron in their diet to support these extra needs. Foods high in iron include red meat, liver, dried beans, whole grains, dark leafy green vegetables, prunes and raisins.

Many pregnant women need additional iron in the form of iron pills, but some do not. Since iron tablets may have annoying side effects, such as constipation or bloating, and can interfere with calcium absorption, it is best not to take them unless you need them.

If you start your pregnancy with a normal hemoglobin level (12 mg percent or higher) you will probably not benefit from routinely taking iron pills in the first half of your pregnancy. Most likely, your doctor will have you get another hemoglobin blood test at 24-28 weeks. If your hemoglobin is low (below 10.5 mg percent), you should start taking iron pills. Otherwise you probably won't need them because your body is getting enough iron from your diet alone.

Herbal Medicines

Consistent, accurate information about the safety and use of herbal medicines in pregnancy is meager because they have not been studied in a scientific manner.

In addition, the concentration of the active ingredients of the herb may vary greatly between manufacturers and even between containers produced by the same manufacturer. The effects of the active chemical compound in one herbal medicine may be altered by diet or other herbal or traditional medicines, leading to unforeseeable results.

Recommendations on the safety of herbal medicines in pregnancy vary considerably in herbal medicine reference books. There appears to be little consensus on a list of herbs considered to be potentially hazardous in pregnancy.

Therefore, with an understanding that absolute accuracy may be a problem in this regard, the following list of herbs is presented as those which may be harmful and should be avoided during pregnancy. In general, it is wise to avoid all herbs and other substances whose effects are totally unknown during pregnancy.

Herbs to be Avoided During Pregnancy:

Aloe-Emodin	Elder Blossoms
Star Anise	Feverfew
Angelica Root	German Chamomile
Arnica	Goldenseal
Barberry Root	Gutu Kola
Benzoin Gum Powder	Juniper Berries
Blood Root	Lily Of The Root
Blue Cohosh	Licorice Root
Buchu Leaves	Lovage
Buckthorn Bark	Mandrake Root
Burdock Root	Misteltoe
Cascara Sagrada	Morman Tea
Coltsfoot	Motherwort
Comfrey	Parsley Root
Damiana	Pennyroyal Leaves
Dong Quai	Wormwood

Medicines and Breastfeeding

After your baby is born, you may also need or want to take some medicines. If you are breastfeeding, the following over-the-counter medicines should be taken with caution, according to the American Academy of Pediatrics: salicylates such as aspirin or bismuth subsalicylate (Pepto-Bismol) and clemastine (Tavist-D).

That is the entire list. The over-the-counter medicines listed on the previous pages (for pregnancy) are considered safe for breast-feeding if taken in appropriate doses.

There are many prescription medications, which should not be taken by breastfeeding mothers (see chapter 7), or should be taken with caution. If you are breastfeeding, discuss this with your doctor.

Diagnostic X-ray Tests

The good news about diagnostic x-ray tests during pregnancy is that the risk of fetal harm has been vastly overrated. The amount of radiation a baby gets during pregnancy from these tests is usually not even close to the level required to cause developmental problems.

For example, it would take about five thousand dental x-ray tests to even approach the level of radiation required to have the potential of causing fetal harm. No one has that many teeth.

The amount of ionizing radiation (the type found in diagnostic x-ray tests and radiation therapy) needed to affect a developing fetus varies somewhat with the gestational age. Regardless of gestational age, however, there is no increased risk to the developing baby of miscarriage, retardation, or malformation at a dose of less than five rads.

From the Doctor's Files

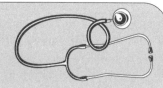

How much radiation is a rad? Well, let's use the example of a pregnant woman who was in a car accident and received serious injuries. She had five x-ray tests of her head, and the total radiation that the fetus was exposed to was 0.00005 rads. That same woman then received two chest x-ray tests, and the baby was exposed to another 0.00004 rads. Lumbar spine tests added an additional 0.001 rad. An intravenous pyelogram to evaluate kidney damage added about 0.25 rads. X-ray tests of her broken legs added about 0.00005 rads.

I am happy to report that both mother and baby survived and are now well. She received many initial diagnostic x-ray studies which, when all added together, resulted in a total fetal dose of 0.25114 rads, far below the five rad threshold for potential fetal injury.

It is not surprising, therefore, that the American College of Radiology has stated, **"No single diagnostic procedure results in a radiation dose significant enough to threaten the well-being of the developing embryo and fetus."**

Basically, if you are pregnant and have a medical problem which requires a diagnostic x-ray study (or two or three) do not be afraid to get it done.

Computed Tomography (CT Scanning)

CT scanning involves multiple exposures of very thin x-ray beams in a 360° circle with computerized interpretations of these images. It has become a very valuable tool for diagnosing a variety of medical problems.

In pregnancy, the most common use of CT scanning is for evaluation of head trauma or brain tumors. The fetal radiation exposure during such a CT is approximately 0.05 rads. A CT scan of the pelvis is occasionally done in pregnancies, resulting in a fetal exposure of about 0.25 rads.

Radiation doses vary somewhat between hospitals, machines, and radiologists. Nonetheless, the amount of radiation getting to a developing baby should not be enough to discourage you or your doctor from having diagnostic x-ray studies done if you need them.

Magnetic Resonance Imaging (MRI)

MRI uses short-term exposure to electromagnetic fields to produce an image. It has been used in pregnancy and currently, there is no evidence that it causes congenital abnormalities or adverse fetal effects.

Chapter 4
Prenatal Genetic Testing and Ultrasound

Nearly all women will be confronted with the opportunity to make a decision regarding genetic testing, relatively early in their pregnancies. It is a difficult, and often disagreeable, subject you may not have thought too much about, or one you may have tried to repress.

Decisions about genetic testing are important and thus require serious thought.

The decision to have genetic studies done is a very personal one. The purpose of getting a test done for most pregnant women is reassurance that their baby does not have any chromosomal or spinal abnormalities or other physical or mental defects. For others, the main purpose of testing is to arrange a timely termination of pregnancy if an abnormality is found.

Genetic Testing

There are several approaches to genetic testing, any of which may be quite appropriate. First, of course, is the option of avoiding the whole subject and deciding not to have any fetal evaluation done. This is a perfectly reasonable choice for many couples who have decided that whatever the condition of the child, they will accept the natural outcome.

If you find yourself in this frame of mind, it is important that you understand the ramifications of having a baby with Down syndrome or neural tube defects prior to making a final decision about genetic testing. This information is obtained by talking to a genetic counselor or a very knowledgeable physician, with a great deal of time for an in-depth discussion.

Family History

Some of us have had relatives with Down syndrome, spina bifida, cystic fibrosis, Tay-Sachs disease, hemophilia, mental retardation, or one of many other disorders which may be hereditary. You may be worried that your risk of having a baby with an inherited disease is high. There are knowledgeable people who can help you, and you should talk with them. They are called genetic counselors.

Your obstetrician may have a smattering of knowledge about genetic disorders. He may even know quite a bit, but even the average genetic counselor knows a great deal more about these problems than do the vast majority of obstetricians. They are also much more thorough in obtaining a detailed family history, which is essential to accurate genetic counseling.

Genetic counselors may be hard to find in smaller communities, but are almost always available in metropolitan areas. Instead of depending on your physician for accurate and in-depth answers to your genetic questions, seek out a genetic counselor. If your doctor refers you to one, most insurance policies will cover the cost.

Down Syndrome

Pregnant women who will be 35 years old or older at the time of delivery have an increased risk of having a baby with a problem known as Down syndrome (also known as Mongolism or Trisomy 21). Babies with Down syndrome always develop mental retardation and often have a variety of major medical problems such as heart defects or intestinal obstruction. They require an enormous amount of physical and emotional care, above and beyond that required by other children.

These children are born with an extra chromosome, which causes all of their troubles. Almost all humans have 46 chromosomes, arranged neatly into 23 nearly identical pairs, which contain all the genetic material responsible for making us the way we are. The extra chromosome (in this case number 21) is easily identifiable on chromosome tests, which can be done on amniotic fluid, fetal blood, or placental specimens.

Down Syndrome Risk

Age	Risk
25	1/1250 (0.08%)
35	1/360 (0.3%)
38	1/175 (0.6%)
40	1/109 (0.9%)
42	1/67 (1.5%)
45	1/33 (3%)

Because of the increasing risk of Down syndrome with advanced age, genetic counseling and testing is routinely offered to pregnant women who are over 34 years old.

Neural Tube Defects

Another major problem for which prenatal testing is offered is that of Neural Tube Defects (NTD). Neural Tube Defects may occur anywhere along the spinal system, including the head. The severity of the problem varies with the location and size of the defect.

The most severe and lethal forms of this disorder affect the baby's head. The most common problem, as well as the easiest to identify, is called anencephaly. Babies born with anencephaly usually have no skull or brain above the level of the ears and mid-forehead. All of these babies die shortly after birth or during pregnancy. This malformation occurs about once in every 1,000 pregnancies.

Other forms of NTDs are less dramatic and grotesque, but usually cause major problems. Open spinal defects (spina bifida) at the level of the waist are the next most frequent NTD and usually result in paralysis below that area, as well as a variety of associated long-term medical problems, often requiring many operations for survival. Mental retardation is another problem that is frequently associated with NTDs. The frequency of babies born with either serious chromosomal abnormalities or NTDs is rather low in the general population (about 3 to 4 per 1000). However, they are among the most frequent major congenital defects, and a variety of tests are available to identify these babies.

Interestingly, the risk of NTDs in Ireland is about 7 per 1000, and the incidence in Japan is less than 1 in 1000. Within the United States, the risks vary considerably, with the highest rates being about 4 per 1000 in New England and in much of the Middle Atlantic region.

Genetic Testing Procedures

Triple Marker Screening

Most pregnant American women, regardless of age, will face a decision about genetic testing between the fifteenth and twentieth week of gestation. A genetic test is available which carries no <u>obvious</u> risks, is relatively cheap, and involves initially nothing more than a routine maternal blood sampling. This test is available nationwide, only under different names. In many parts of the country, this test is called a

Triple Marker Screen (TMS). Other names for the same test include Multiple Marker Screen, Maternal Alpha-Fetoprotein, and Triple Screen.

The purpose of the TMS test is to identify those women who have a higher than usual risk of having a baby with either a Neural Tube Defect or major chromosome abnormality (most commonly Down syndrome). It is not a diagnostic test. No matter how abnormal the test result, a diagnosis can only be made by either ultrasound or amniocentesis. Likewise, a normal result doesn't guarantee a totally normal baby, although the likelihood is very high.

In order for this test to be accurate, the gestational age of the pregnancy must be known, as this data is an integral part of determining the results. The test is only done between 15 and 20 weeks (from the last menstrual period) of pregnancy. If a woman and her doctor believe that she is 16 weeks along, but in reality, she is only in her 14th week, the test results will be wrong and may falsely indicate a high risk for abnormalities. Likewise, if the baby in fact has Down syndrome, and an error is made in determining the gestational age, a normal test result may be falsely reassuring. This is one reason why routine ultrasound in the second trimester is so very important.

When the alpha-fetoprotein part of the test is abnormally high, it indicates an increased risk for a variety of pregnancy-related problems, including future risk for an undergrown baby, twins, premature labor or delivery, preeclampsia (formally called toxemia of pregnancy), placental separation, stillbirth, NTDs, and a variety of other fetal abnormalities which are quite rare. The higher the result, the higher the risk for any of these problems. Even so, for women with abnormally high test results, the risk for open spinal defects remains less than 5%. This part of the test may come back falsely elevated if you have vaginal bleeding in the two weeks prior to the test. Be sure to tell your doctor about any bleeding you have during this time.

When the TMS results suggest a higher risk of a neural tube defect, an ultrasound exam needs to be done. First, clarification of the gestational age is needed to verify the accuracy of the TMS test. Secondly, since a variety of pregnancy problems may lead to an abnormal test, these are important to identify. Twins, fetal death, gross fetal malformations, and placental abnormalities can all be easily seen, and would explain an abnormal test result. Finally, the ultrasonographer can look at the baby's spine and head very carefully, in an attempt to identify a Neural Tube Defect.

When the ultrasound exam shows no defects, with the due date being accurate and no apparent explanation of the high test result, a second TMS test should be done. If this result comes back normal, no further evaluation is needed, as the likelihood of fetal defects or future pregnancy problems is very small.

Detection of Down Syndrome

If the TMS results indicate an increased risk for Down syndrome, a decision needs to be made about getting an amniocentesis done, because that is the only test which can definitely determine the baby's status. Repeating the blood test is of no benefit. If the amniocentesis results then come back normal, no further testing is needed. The baby should not be expected to have other problems.

Decisions, Decisions

Your obstetrician may strongly suggest that you get this blood test done. However, he may not tell you about the significant negatives built into the entire genetic testing system.

The main problem with the TMS test is the great anxiety which naturally develops when the results come back abnormal. After further testing, more than 95% of those babies turn out to be normal, and thus many parents go through a great deal of unnecessary anguish.

If you know that your anxiety level will skyrocket if you have an abnormal TMS test, you should give serious thought to not getting this "harmless" test done, in spite of your doctor's urging. **Remember, these genetic decisions are yours, not his.**

A better way to approach genetic testing concerns is to have an ultrasound exam done first, at about 16 to 18 weeks. An accurate ultrasound evaluation will identify more than 90% of babies with neural tube defects. If your baby's spinal system appears normal, half the reason for getting a TMS test has just been eliminated.

A normal ultrasound evaluation cannot rule out Down syndrome, however, certain positive findings are suspicious if present and may convince you that a TMS test (or even genetic amniocentesis) should be done.

Findings which may indicate a baby with
Down syndrome:

- Short thigh and/or upper arm bones.
- Abnormal shape of the head.
- Bowel which appears whiter than usual.
- Thickened skin fold in the back of the neck.
- Abnormal heart.
- Large or absent stomach.
- Extra fluid seen in both kidneys

If your initial inclination was to avoid the TMS test, but your baby has one or more of these unusual findings, you may want to reassess your decision.

Chorionic Villus Sampling (CVS)

The earliest genetic test that can be done in pregnancy is chorionic villus sampling (see figure 1). This test is usually done between 9 and 12 weeks of gestation. During this procedure, microscopic bits of placenta are removed, either by a tube placed through the cervix into the uterus, or by a needle through the abdomen or vagina. Placement of the collecting tube or needle needs to be exact, and ultrasound is used simultaneously to locate the placenta.

Figure 1
Chorionic Villus Sampling (CVS)

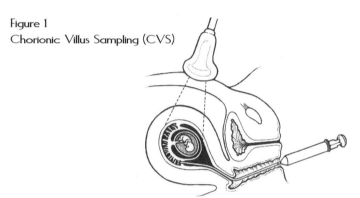

The advantage of CVS is that it is done early and the test results are back quickly. If termination of pregnancy is chosen, it can be done in the first trimester, when this procedure is relatively simple and can easily be done on an outpatient basis. Another advantage is that the good results also come back early.

Disadvantages of CVS compared to amniocentesis:

- No information regarding neural tube defects can be obtained by CVS.
- The test is considerably more expensive.
- It must be performed by a doctor (usually a perinatologist) with a great deal of training and experience. These doctors are nearly always found only at university medical centers, which for many people means traveling a considerable distance.
- There is an increased risk of miscarriage.

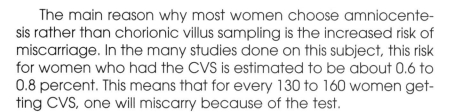

The main reason why most women choose amniocentesis rather than chorionic villus sampling is the increased risk of miscarriage. In the many studies done on this subject, this risk for women who had the CVS is estimated to be about 0.6 to 0.8 percent. This means that for every 130 to 160 women getting CVS, one will miscarry because of the test.

Genetic Amniocentesis

The most frequently chosen diagnostic genetic test in pregnancy is the amniocentesis (also called an amnio), usually done at 15 or 16 weeks. In this procedure, a needle is placed through the mother's abdomen into the uterus, and a sample of amniotic fluid is removed (see figure 2). It sounds quite painful, but according to nearly all of our patients, it feels like getting blood drawn, only in the abdomen. An ultrasound exam is done either just prior to or often during the procedure for maximum safety and efficiency. Some doctors use local anesthesia to numb the mother's abdominal skin, others do not.

Figure 2
Amniocentesis

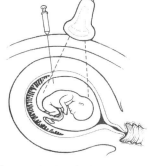

The amount of amniotic fluid removed is usually 15 to 25 cc. A tablespoon is 30 cc. The loss of this amount of fluid is of no importance to the baby, who is surrounded by 200 to 400 cc of fluid at that time. Floating in the amniotic fluid are many cells, originating from the baby, and these can be grown in tissue cultures in the genetics laboratory. This latter process presently takes anywhere from 7 to 10 days. A small sample of the fluid is also tested for alpha-fetoprotein levels, which is a test for open spinal defects.

Amniocentesis is not a risk-free procedure. About one out of every 300 women who have this test done will have a miscarriage from the trauma or an infection caused by inserting the needle in the uterus.

Serious injury to the baby from the needle is rare, but it can and does occur if the needle is inserted into critical organs such as the liver or brain. It is reassuring to know, however, that even when the baby is stuck with the needle, serious injuries are very unlikely. The use of ultrasound to direct the needle to a clear space in the uterus has reduced the trauma risk dramatically.

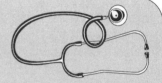

From the Doctor's Files

Actually, the person who seems to suffer the most during an amniocentesis is usually the baby's father, who has come along to be supportive. We have had far more problems with woozy fathers than traumatized mothers or babies.   (I watched one literally crawl out of the room during his wife's test.)

One husband, a dentist no less, became lightheaded and almost fainted. This caused his wife to laugh so much that she could not stop, and I had to remove the needle because it was moving around so much from her laughter that I thought it might hit the baby.

After an amniocentesis, there is usually a small amount of uterine cramping or mild tenderness in the area of the needle stick, not unlike the discomfort of a vaccination. Women can return to normal activity for the rest of the day. About 1 percent of women having this test will experience a small amount of clear fluid discharge from the vagina for a day or two. This rarely results in further troubles and no treatment is needed.

Ultrasound

A review of the world's history of obstetrical care will show three technological advances which have had a dramatic and positive impact on the health of pregnant women and their babies.

The earliest was the invention of obstetric forceps in the 17th century by a member of a family of English physicians, the Chamberlens. Prior to that time, if a baby was too big to be born spontaneously, death was the inevitable outcome for the baby and a frequent outcome for the mother as well. With the advent of the Chamberlen forceps, many mothers' and babies' lives were saved. Many of you owe your very existence to the invention of the obstetric forceps and the lifesaving maneuvers done to deliver you or one of your ancestors.

The next major advance was the invention of general anesthesia in the 1800's, which allowed cesarean sections to be considered as a rational option for delivery. It is fair to say that since then, millions of pregnant women and their babies have survived birth because they underwent a cesarean section rather than facing the more natural, but often tragic, consequences of a severely complicated vaginal delivery.

The third and latest great medical advance in obstetric care has been the introduction of diagnostic ultrasound. Until the 1960's, the only imaging technique available in pregnancy was with radiographic (x-ray) studies. These were not only minimally helpful in the amount of knowledge that was obtained, but were also potentially dangerous, due to radiation exposure.

85

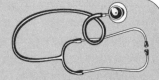

From the Doctor's Files

As a medical student at the University of Colorado in 1970, I had the very good fortune of being a student of Dr. Kenneth Gottesfeld, an obstetrician, who was one of the pioneers in the area of diagnostic obstetric ultrasound. At that time, what we "saw" with our machines was a still photo of a series of white dots on a black background. It was our job to make some sense out of what we were seeing. We could identify the placental location, the fetal skull, and various other fetal bones and major anatomic structures.

The technology of diagnostic ultrasound machines has improved far beyond anything we dreamed of in 1970. If Dr. Gottesfeld were alive today, he would marvel at what we can see and measure: blood flow through the tiny blood vessels in fetal brains, fetal eye movement in sleep and excited states, motion of heart valves no bigger than a comma on this page, and distances between spinal processes measured in tenths of millimeters, just to name a few.

When You Get An Ultrasound Done

There are few thrills in life that compare to seeing your baby by ultrasound for the first time. The procedure is fairly simple. You are usually asked to arrive in the ultrasound room with a relatively full bladder and lie down on a table, while the sonographer (often called an ultrasound technician) places a small mechanical device, called a transducer, on your abdomen. The sound waves emitted from the transducer bounce off whatever is inside you and return through the transducer into the computer in the ultrasound machine. An image can then be shown on a screen, much like a television screen. Other than the possible discomfort of an overfull bladder, there are really no other discomforts involved.

Most sonographers are compassionate enough to use warmed gel on your abdomen for the scan. Some, however, still use cold gel, which is mildly annoying. You should ask to have warm gel if possible. It's a lot nicer. (While we're on the subject, you can also ask your doctor to warm the lubricant he has in his office. Simply by placing his tube of lubricant on a heating pad, he can show you a little kindness when he does your pelvic exams.)

The sonographer should take the time to show you around your baby. She can point out details, such as fingers and toes, quite easily. If, at the end of your scan, you feel as though you have not seen enough of the baby, tell the sonographer. If there are specific things you want to see, you may need to speak up. Don't allow yourself to be intimidated.

If you are now pregnant, the likelihood that you will get an ultrasound exam sometime during your pregnancy is quite high, probably about 70 to 75 percent. There are 23 standard indications for the use of diagnostic ultrasound, according to the National Institute of Health. It is hard not to qualify for an ultrasound exam if you are pregnant.

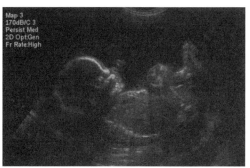

Safety of Diagnostic Ultrasound

There have been literally thousands of scientific studies done, utilizing information from millions of babies and animals, resulting in billions of bits of data, all in an attempt to show that diagnostic obstetric ultrasound is harmful to developing babies. They have failed to do so.

On the subject of the safety of diagnostic obstetric ultrasound, the American Institute of Ultrasound in Medicine has stated, "No confirmed biologic effects on patients or instrument operators... have ever been reported."

Videotaping and Pictures

Nearly all women getting a complete ultrasound exam will be offered a picture of their baby at the end of the scan, but not all institutions allow videotaping of the scan. Many radiologists who are in charge of making that kind of decision don't want parents taping the ultrasound exam because of their fear of being sued if they fail to identify a fetal malformation.

Nearly all recently built ultrasound machines have the capacity to videotape, and some radiologists tape the entire scan for review later. You should be allowed to tape at least part of the ultrasound scan, if not all of it. It is your baby, isn't it? When you are making an appointment to have an ultrasound, make sure that you tell them that you are bringing a blank videotape along and expect to use it. If enough people begin to do this, after a while, the radiologists will begin to get the idea.

Your Full Bladder

The most common complaint about obstetric ultrasound is the need for a full bladder. It can be very distressing to have someone putting a transducer on a bladder that feels like it is about to explode. We suggest that if your bladder is uncomfortably full early in the exam, ask the sonographer to do those things that require a full bladder first, and then stop, so you can get up and go to the bathroom. Most exams done after 24 weeks do not require a full bladder. An ultrasound is so much more enjoyable with an empty bladder.

Bonding

As soon as most women realize that they are pregnant, they begin an emotional attachment to their baby, known as bonding. They feel many changes happening in their body, not all of which are pleasant, but all of which tell them that their baby is growing inside them. It is a time of miraculous changes.

The baby's father does not feel any of these things, and although he may also be happy and excited about the new baby-to-be, he doesn't sense anything different yet. That all changes abruptly when the father sees his baby on the ultrasound screen. This usually results in a dramatic change in his perception of the pregnancy.

When getting an ultrasound, you should make certain that the important people in your life have an opportunity to see the baby with you. This may include older children. Don't let the sonographer or the radiologist make you be there alone. It is your right to have the father of the baby there with you, and it should be the sonographer's duty to make sure that he is invited.

From the Nurse's Notes

Bringing very young children is usually a bad idea. Their attention span is very short, and their presence is usually more trouble than the parents bargain for. We should also mention that we discourage bringing pets ever since a patient of ours brought her mother and her cat to watch her ultrasound scan. Some people can get carried away with bonding.

Purposes of an Ultrasound Scan

Calculating a Due Date

Most young American women can recall within a few days when their last menstrual period began. This date has always been the basis of determining a subsequent due date 40 weeks later. However, with the use of the fetal measurements seen by early ultrasound, we now know that 10-15 percent of women who were "sure" of their last menstrual period need to have their due date corrected by at least 10 days.

The measurements obtained by an ultrasound exam in the first trimester are accurate to within three to four days.

Most pregnant women who receive routine ultrasound scans will have them done 16 to 20 weeks after their last menstrual period. At that time, the test is usually accurate within 10 days. After that time, as babies grow, ultrasound measurements become progressively less accurate in determining a due date.

Twin Pregnancy

Every pregnant woman wonders if she is going to have twins. By using ultrasound, the number of babies present can be easily identified in seconds. Rarely will a sonographer miss seeing a second baby.

Fetal Evaluation

In addition to wondering how many babies are growing inside them, all mothers want to know if their babies are normal. The use of an ultrasound scan can help a great deal in allaying the fear of having an abnormal baby.

About one baby in 50 will be born with a significant physical abnormality. Some of these abnormalities are easily seen at birth, such as an open spinal defect or cleft lip. Others, such as certain small heart defects, only become apparent when the baby becomes sick or a heart murmur is heard.

When a normal-appearing fetus is carefully evaluated by a registered sonographer, using standard techniques after 16 weeks, the likelihood that the fetus has a life-threatening abnormality which has been missed, is very small.

Identification of Placental Position

The placenta, often called the afterbirth, is very easy to identify with ultrasound. Usually, its position is of no great importance, but occasionally it is.

A common error made by inexperienced sonographers occurs when, during a routine ultrasound at 16 to 20 weeks, the placenta is noted to be implanted low in the uterus, near the cervix but not covering it. This information frightens the doctor, and he may tell his pregnant patient to avoid intercourse, get off her feet, stop working, or even that she will need a cesarean section for delivery. That may be a gross over-reaction to a normal situation.

Early in pregnancy, the placental position frequently may be seen as being low, almost at the edge of the cervical opening. This is no cause for alarm. The natural course of events is that the placenta will gradually "migrate" up the wall of the uterus, away from the cervix. Ninety-five percent of the time, if another scan is done 10 to 16 weeks later, the placenta will be seen as being much higher and away from the cervix (see fig 3). The placenta does not actually move, but appears higher because of lengthening of the uterine muscle, just above the cervix, putting more distance between the cervix and placenta.

Figure 3
Low-lying Placenta

16 Weeks   30 Weeks

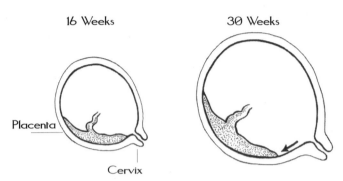

Placenta

Cervix

Only when the placenta actually covers the cervix in early pregnancy is there cause for concern. If your doctor tells you a lot of worrisome things about the position of your placenta, make sure he clarifies whether the placenta is just "low" and not really a problem, or if it truly covers the cervical opening, which may cause bleeding problems later in your pregnancy.

Fetal Gender

From the point of view of your doctor or sonographer, the least important piece of information found on an obstetric ultrasound scan may be the sex of your baby. From your point of view, it may be the only thing you remember seeing and the most important part of the whole scan.

Determination of fetal sex gets easier as the fetus gets bigger. Even so, our ability to identify the gender even with a term baby is not accurate 100 percent of the time. Positions of the baby's legs and the amount of amniotic fluid play an important role in visualization. At 16 to 20 weeks, when most routine ultrasounds are done, sex determination can some-times be difficult, even for very experienced sonographers.

Fetal Growth

A frequent reason why many pregnant women get an ultrasound exam done is because the baby seems to be growing either too poorly or perhaps too well. There is a wide range of normal-sized babies at term, ranging from about 5 1/2 pounds to 10 pounds.

When a condition exists which significantly reduces the flow of nutrients and oxygen to the developing baby, growth slows down and this baby is at risk of having a lot of problems. An ultrasound evaluation of fetal growth, usually done in the last three months of pregnancy, can identify these babies.

Often, when a baby at term seems very large, the doctor orders an ultrasound to get an idea of its size. This is usually a bad idea (except in cases of diabetes, see chapter 8), because it leads to many unnecessary cesarean sections. Estimated fetal weight by ultrasound is not as accurate as we would like, with a range of error of about 12 percent. This correlates to a two-pound range for an eight-pound baby. Knowing that a baby is large often discourages mothers and doctors, and leads to premature decisions to do cesarean sections.

Just as babies' sizes vary greatly, mothers' pelvic dimensions also vary greatly. We are frequently amazed at the large size of babies pushed out by small women. Larger babies take more time and effort to deliver. A positive attitude toward delivery on the part of both mother and doctor can be very beneficial in the course of these longer labors.

Risk For Premature Delivery

Preterm labor and subsequent preterm delivery are among the most common serious problems pregnant women and their babies face. Some of the causes of preterm labor can be identified on a routine scan at 16 to 20 weeks.

It is becoming clear that the ultrasonic finding of a shortened uterine cervix in the second trimester identifies many women who are at high risk for developing preterm labor. By proper evaluation and treatment of these women, their preterm deliveries can often be postponed for several weeks.

The opposite finding is also helpful. Quite often, a woman presents to the labor and delivery area with frequent contractions between 24 and 36 weeks of her pregnancy, but her cervix remains closed. The question is whether or not to be aggressive in treating these contractions. If her cervix is more than 3 cm long, the likelihood of progressive preterm labor at that time is small. If her cervix is shorter, the risks are higher. Therefore, ultrasound evaluation of cervical length aids in our diagnosis and treatment of this frequent problem.

Identification of the Baby's Position

One of the easiest things to see during a scan is the baby's position. Babies do a lot of spinning around and change their position frequently before the 9th month. Until then, their position is of little importance. (See chapter 10 for discussion of breech babies.)

Qualifications and Experience of the Sonographer

The ability of sonographers to detect fetal abnormalities varies tremendously. In some studies, only 10 to 15 percent of the major fetal defects were identified. On others, 75 to 80 percent of all defects are found. Why is this?

Unfortunately, a major variable in the accuracy of your baby's evaluation is the knowledge and experience of the person who is holding the ultrasound transducer on your pregnant abdomen.

It would be nice if all sonographers were as well trained and thorough as they are in most major medical centers, but, sadly, they are not. Many pregnant women are getting inadequate, often inaccurate ultrasound testing done by poorly trained doctors in their offices or by inappropriately supervised personnel who are not following standard practices. This can lead to disastrous results.

From the Doctor's Files
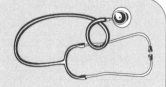

In the month of September in 1990, I saw two pregnant women whose stories illustrate this problem perfectly. Betty, a very pleasant, very heavy woman, came from a small town near our clinic. She had three children at home and, then in her fourth pregnancy, she went to see her doctor because of some light vaginal bleeding that she was having about 18 weeks into her pregnancy. She had not yet felt the baby move.

Her doctor had an ultrasound machine in his office, and when he looked at Betty's baby, he saw no fetal heartbeat. He told Betty that, unfortunately, her baby had died and the light bleeding was the earliest sign of an impending miscarriage. Betty was heartbroken.

She was referred to me by her doctor for an induction of labor because he was unfamiliar with termination of pregnancy in the second trimester. I always verify a diagnosis of fetal death or malformation myself, so Betty, her husband, Ron, and I walked down the hall to one of our ultrasound rooms. As she lay down on the table, she turned her head away from the monitor so she would not have to see her dead baby again. Once was enough for her.

I placed the ultrasound transducer on Betty's generous abdomen and was surprised and delighted to see that her baby was very much alive with a normal heartbeat. Betty was ecstatic, but Ron was really upset. "Why did Dr. B tell us our baby was dead?" he asked. My answer was simple. "Because he made a mistake."

Betty went on to have a normal pregnancy and a healthy baby. The problem her doctor had was that her layers of abdominal fat obscured his ability to see the baby. And, because he did not have sufficient experience with ultrasound, he assumed that his not seeing a heartbeat in this situation meant that there was no heartbeat.

Later that same month, Rhonda came to see me, desiring a second opinion. She was pregnant with her second baby and had recently had an ultrasound done at a nearby small hospital. The hospital's sonographer doing the scan did them once a week and did not have a great deal of experience in obstetric ultrasound.

At the end of Rhonda's original scan, the radiologist told her that her baby had hydrocephaly (too much water in the brain), a very serious problem. When she came to see me, she said, "I don't know, but he really didn't seem to know what he was talking about." So, she wanted another opinion.

On that day, Rhonda and I looked at her baby very carefully, and I could see no evidence of hydrocephaly or any other malformation. Rhonda was relieved and happy, and went on to have a healthy baby.

These kinds of situations are very disturbing. I wonder how many tragedies have occurred and how many panic-stricken parents have suffered needlessly because of the diagnosis of problems that, in fact, did not exist.

The American Institute of Ultrasound and Medicine along with the American College of Obstetrics and Gynecology have set minimum standards for a complete obstetric ultrasound exam. When you get an ultrasound done in your pregnancy, you should make certain that the person doing the scan is familiar with and follows the minimum standards.

Fetal Abnormalities: After Detection, Then What?

Working in a high-risk obstetric center, we have seen more than our fair share of babies with abnormalities that were discovered during an ultrasound exam. The wide range of possible findings and diagnoses is absolutely mind-numbing. For instance, there are presently 212 different types of skeletal disorders which babies can have at birth. It is not the purpose of this chapter to cover all aspects of individual birth defects, so we will focus on two basic principles.

Principle 1: Early identification of major fetal abnormalities will allow parents the opportunity to choose whether or not to continue the pregnancy.

This principle is particularly important because it touches on major ethical issues in medical care. There is currently a debate within the American medical care system on whether all pregnant women should be offered routine obstetric ultrasound in the second trimester.

Failure to offer routine obstetric ultrasound prior to the time of viability (23 or 24 weeks) effectively limits access to appropriate fetal evaluation and the possibility of abortion for fetal abnormalities. This becomes a significant intrusion on the woman's autonomy and runs contrary to the ethical obligation of the obstetrician to serve as his patient's advocate for optimum medical care.

Principle 2: The identification of a fetal malformation is not always a bad thing. Sometimes, babies benefit greatly because of the identification of that abnormal finding.

Identification of some surgically correctable defects will allow for a much more intelligent birth plan and neonatal care. These plans can be life-saving.

What If?

We do not have the ability to identify all fetal abnormalities. As our ability to diagnose genetic disorders improves, our ability to know what to do about these problems, during pregnancy and beyond, sometimes becomes less clear.

Ethical considerations and legal restrictions become paramount when a baby is found to have a major abnormality. When the abnormality is definitely lethal, the decision-making process is more clearly defined. Termination of pregnancy, also known as therapeutic abortion, is nearly always the route chosen, and legal concerns are minimal.

The course is not as clear when abnormalities such as Down syndrome or spina bifida are found. Usually, these babies survive infancy, sometimes with a great deal of surgical help. Some will be profoundly retarded, others less so or not at all. During pregnancy it is not possible to predict their eventual outcome.

The decision to terminate a pregnancy or to bring a child into the world with a debilitating problem is as difficult a decision as a woman could ever have. One thing is quite clear, however, the decision is <u>hers</u>. It is not her doctor's, her mother's, or even her husband's.

Prior to making the decision whether or not to terminate a pregnancy, the couple needs to know as much as possible about raising children with a problem, and also what a termination of pregnancy entails.

Chapter 5

Pain Relief for Labor and Delivery

There are many wonderful joys of pregnancy and having children. However, for many pregnant women, the fear of the expected pain during the process of labor and delivery overshadows what could be a deeply gratifying experience. You don't need to let this happen to you: **There are good ways to reduce the pain of childbirth.**

Causes of Pain in Labor

When labor begins, the uterus, which is 95 percent smooth muscle, contracts and relaxes in a rhythmic pattern. At first these contractions are several minutes apart and then gradually become more frequent, until they are two to three minutes apart and last about 45 to 60 seconds.

As the uterus contracts, the cervix gradually thins and opens as the baby's head pushes against it. Some of the pain of labor is due to these changes in the cervix, but not all.

As the baby's head slowly comes down into the birth canal it stretches most of the muscles in the pelvis. If these muscles are tense, there is great pain. If these muscles are relaxed, there is much less pain.

You cannot control the actions of your smooth muscles. However, most other muscles in your body, called striated muscles, are under your control. You can contract or relax them at will.

There are many of these striated muscles in your pelvis, some deep inside the vagina (or birth canal), and some around the opening of the vagina and rectum.

Once the cervix is completely dilated, there is no more pain arising from it and the sensations of labor now come from the lower part of the vagina and rectum. Muscles and other tissues are stretching to their maximum to allow for passage of the baby's head.

All these dramatic changes taking place do not happen without some element of pain. Fortunately for you, there are several methods of relieving that pain which can be very helpful.

Non-Medical Pain Relief

By far, the most natural of all the types of pain relief is that of muscle relaxation. By controlling the pelvic muscles and allowing them to relax, you can dramatically reduce the intensity of the pain of labor. This takes work, time, and effort, and most of that work must be done long before labor begins.

It is well known that anxiety leads to tense muscles resulting in pain. Tense pelvic muscles trying to resist the powerful muscles of the laboring uterus result in long, painful labors.

This doesn't have to happen to you, especially if you begin learning and practicing muscle relaxation techniques early in pregnancy. By consciously relaxing your muscles during contractions in the first stage of labor (i.e., until complete cervical dilatation), and in between pushing efforts thereafter, the excessive muscle tension will not be there to cause pain, and the baby will be born more easily and comfortably.

The technique of muscle relaxation allows muscle tone throughout the body to be reduced to a minimum (See appendix I). A state of complete muscle relaxation leads to a dramatic reduction in anxiety as well. More information on this subject can be found on the internet at www.Hypnobirthing.com

From the Nurse's Notes

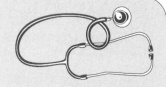

You cannot effectively relax in labor without having practiced it at home. This is something almost any woman can do. All it requires is some time alone in a comfortable, quiet place and the willingness to work at it for a few months. If you have access to relaxation tapes or a hypnotherapist, the process of relaxation can be even easier.

Some hospitals have Jacuzzi baths in their labor and delivery area, which can be very helpful in getting your muscles to relax and thus relieve much of the pain of labor. These are safe, even when the membranes have ruptured.

Additionally, having a support person present throughout your labor can be very helpful. The one-on-one attention you receive from a supportive partner lowers stress and anxiety considerably. This person can be a helpful husband, a close friend, a hired (or volunteer) support person, or a midwife.

Anything that provides emotional or physical relaxation and decreases anxiety will provide some measure of pain relief during labor. Some women find that listening to relaxing music or rocking in a rocking chair, holding a favorite stuffed bear, or even sitting in a lotus position helps them get into a state of relaxation. **Natural methods of relaxation can be very effective for pain relief in labor.**

Pain Medication (Analgesics)

Most laboring women receiving pain medication in labor will notice a moderate reduction in the intensity of their pain. For many, this is all they need to cope. For others, it is inadequate.

Drugs given for pain are given either intravenously or by intramuscular injection. In addition to pain relief, they often produce some drowsiness, euphoria, or nausea.

Years ago, many women in labor were given massive amounts of pain medication. It worked to control the pain, but frequently the babies were born so sedated that they did not breathe on their own until the medicine wore off. The dosages of medicine we use today are much lower, so concern about sedated babies is rarely warranted.

If a baby is lethargic due to maternal pain medication, another medicine, called Narcan, will resolve the problem quickly. Therefore, there is little reason to avoid pain medicine in labor for fear of causing harm to the baby.

Regional Anesthesia

There are two basic types of regional anesthesia; spinals and epidurals. The results are similar: no pain from the chest down, and a mind that is clear and alert.

Both require a needle to be inserted in your back at about waist level. Local anesthesia is often used in the skin on the back, making the process very tolerable.

Spinal anesthesia means that an anesthetic drug is placed through the needle into the spinal fluid. The needle is then removed and you are rolled onto your back. Within a few minutes, a feeling of warmth starts climbing up your legs, and shortly thereafter, you are numb from about the chest down.

Epidurals are somewhat different from spinals in that after the needle enters a space outside of the area of the spinal fluid, a long skinny tube is pushed through the needle into that space, and then the needle is removed. The remaining tube is taped to your back and anesthetic medicine is then injected. This medicine coats the nerves, and thereafter, no pain is felt below your chest. The level and intensity of anesthesia with an epidural is adjustable, depending on the concentration and amount of medicine given.

Placing an epidural takes more time and expertise than a spinal and many smaller hospitals do not have doctors capable of doing them.

Epidural Anesthesia

For the laboring woman requiring pain relief, nothing is more effective than a well-placed epidural anesthetic. It provides excellent and often total pain relief, not only for labor but also for delivery. The medication that is used, usually some type of local anesthetic, appears to have no sedating effect on the baby or mother, and the pain relief achieved can be continued for many hours. It is truly the "Cadillac of anesthesias," and most women who get it are extremely delighted and relieved.

Unfortunately, epidural anesthesia has its significant potential drawbacks. It may slow the progress of labor, cause a serious drop in maternal blood pressure, lead to a worrisome fetal heart-rate tracing, increase the baby's temperature, and reduce the strength of pushing efforts. The result of these common problems is an increase in unnecessary forceps deliveries and cesarean sections.

Most obstetricians don't tell their patients about these problems. In many American hospitals, the majority of women in labor have epidural anesthesia. Many obstetricians encourage epidurals in labor, in part because it provides them some control over the timing of the delivery, and in part because they can also control the woman's response to pain. Being in control is an underlying issue for many obstetricians, and epidural anesthesia is the perfect vehicle for that control.

> The unwanted, potential complications
> of epidural anesthesia can be minimized if:
>
> - Labor is well-established and your cervix is dilated five centimeters or more.
> - Other methods of pain relief are used first.
> - You are well hydrated prior to the procedure.
> - The medication used in the epidural anesthesia allows for some sensation of pelvic pressure, since a total lack of sensation almost guarantees problems with the pushing stage of labor.

Spinal Anesthesia

In some hospitals, anesthesiologists can give laboring women a "walking spinal". For the laboring woman this involves having a needle placed in the spinal fluid and narcotics injected, rather than a local anesthetic. This allows for pain relief with the ability to be more mobile. It does, however, come with a small risk of a post-spinal headache.

Spinal anesthesia, which makes a woman's pelvis numb, may be excellent in those cases where forceps or vacuum delivery is necessary, but otherwise will not be useful in labor because the duration of anesthesia is too short.

Paracervical Block

During the first stage of labor, much of the pain is due to the stretching of the cervix. The nerve fibers to the cervix can be anesthetized with a well-placed needle and local anesthesia. This may be ideal for women with fast labors. The medicine only lasts 45 to 60 minutes, however, and may be technically difficult to administer after the cervix is 8 cm dilated. Rarely, serious problems have occurred when the medicine has caused the baby's heart rate to drop, and for that reason most physicians don't use this technique anymore.

Pudendal Nerve Block

The nerve that picks up sensations from the perineum is called the pudendal nerve. If it can be anesthetized, a woman can have a nearly painless delivery. A pudendal block involves having a needle placed in the vagina just prior to delivery and local anesthetic injected in the area of the pudendal nerve. Some doctors are very adept at it and thus can provide you with good pain relief for delivery. It is not useful for the pain of labor.

Local Anesthesia

As the baby's head is stretching the tissues of the opening of the vagina, sometimes an episiotomy is suggested (see Chapter 6). This requires local anesthetic injected into the skin between the vagina and rectum. It stings for about 15 seconds but then the area becomes numb so that an episiotomy or suturing of a laceration can be done painlessly.

Anesthesia for Cesarean Sections

Every operation requires some kind of pain relief. For cesarean sections, there are two main types: general and regional anesthesia. Both have their advantages and disadvantages under different circumstances. Very rarely, under the most dire circumstances, is a cesarean done with only the use of local anesthetic injected into the area which is going to be incised. Even more rarely, have these operations been performed successfully using nothing but hypnosis for pain relief.

General Anesthesia

If you are under general anesthesia, you are "put to sleep." The anesthesiologist (or anesthetist) gives you some medicine through the intravenous tubing, and in a few minutes you are unconscious and feel no pain. After the operation is over, you gradually wake up, either in the operating room or the recovery room.

When you are under general anesthesia, you will not be able to breathe on your own, and you lose the gag reflex, which normally keeps saliva and digested food out of your lungs. Therefore, nearly everyone given general anesthesia will have a tube placed in her mouth and down into her windpipe (trachea). This is done immediately after you are put to sleep, so you should not feel it.

There are some good things about having general anesthesia for a cesarean section. First and foremost, general anesthesia takes little time to start, and this makes it ideal for circumstances where time is an important factor. In emergency situations, general anesthesia is almost always the best choice. Luckily, these happen infrequently.

Under general anesthesia, you feel nothing. You also see nothing, hear nothing, and know nothing. After surgery, patients who receive general anesthesia wake up slowly in the recovery room and go through a groggy stage, which usually lasts a few hours. Often, nausea and vomiting occur during this time. Pain relief in the form of intravenous or intramuscular medicine reduces, but almost never totally eliminates, the pain.

As you become more alert, you can control your pain relief medicine simply by pressing a button. A small dose of pain medication goes into your vein through the intravenous tubing, being controlled by a pump (PCA pump), which limits the amount and frequency of the dosages.

Pain relief for the first day or so after surgery with general anesthesia is done this way. After that, pain pills usually suffice. Some doctors still use shots (intramuscular injections) for pain medicine, but these are not as quick or reliable as the PCA pump.

Nausea can be a big problem after general anesthesia. There is medicine for that, too, of course. In addition, a sore throat is a common side effect because of the tube, which was inserted down the throat during surgery.

Many women want general anesthesia because they are afraid of complications from a spinal or epidural anesthetic. In reality, general anesthesia has more potential for serious complications than does regional anesthesia, although both are quite safe in the hands of an experienced anesthesiologist or anesthetist.

Regional Anesthesia

During surgery with spinal anesthesia, you usually feel nothing except occasional movement or mild pressure. This is also true of most epidurals, but, in rare instances, an epidural doesn't "take" completely, and there is a small area which, for some reason, doesn't become completely numb.

One of the nicest aspects of regional anesthesia is that you get to see your baby right after it is born. That is always a special moment, and with this kind of anesthesia, both mother and father can share it together. Usually, the nurses bring the baby over and you can touch your baby even while the operation is still going on. There is always a surgical sheet propped up near chest level, which keeps you from seeing the operation itself.

Another nice thing about this kind of anesthesia is that after the medicine is administered, another dose of a longer-acting pain-relief medicine can be given, which results in an almost pain-free existence for 6-24 hours. As the first day after surgery is almost always the most painful, this pain-free time is truly one of the great benefits of regional anesthesia. Feeling and strength quickly returns to the legs, but pain is minimal.

The longer-term recovery is also better. With regional anesthesia, very few women suffer from post-operative gas pains, which are all too frequent after general anesthesia.

From the Doctor's Files

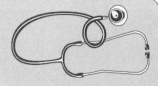

A common worry people have about spinal and epidural anesthesia is being paralyzed afterwards. This almost never happens. I have never seen it, nor has it occurred in any of the 5000 or so cesareans which have occurred in the hospitals where I have worked.

As mentioned, the most common problem after spinal anesthesia is a spinal headache. This occurs infrequently, about two to three days afterward. It is a very severe headache, which is characteristically relieved when lying flat, and made worse by standing up. It can be cured immediately and completely by the use of an epidural procedure known as a "blood patch", which is just like having an epidural anesthetic, except instead of injecting an anesthetic, the doctor injects some of your own blood. If you are unlucky enough to get a spinal headache, ask for an epidural patch.

This is a lot of information on the risks and benefits of different types of anesthesia for cesarean section. It is very difficult in a crisis or semi-crisis situation in labor to calmly discuss this and make a rational decision. Therefore, we suggest discussing this with your doctor well before labor starts. Between the two of you, you can calmly decide what kind of anesthesia would be best for you if you need a cesarean section. **Unless there is some very good reason to the contrary, you would be wise to request either spinal or epidural anesthesia.**

Chapter 6

Labor and Delivery

Even in our highly technological society, birth and death remain the two most significant natural events in our lives. Creating a new life and bringing that baby into the world force us to appreciate our connection to the natural world.

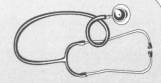

From the Nurse's Notes

The woman who is in labor for the first time quickly comes to the realization that she has entered a world she has never known before. None of the prenatal videotapes, books, or classes can adequately communicate the intensity of labor and delivery or the exhilaration of giving birth.

It is precisely the intensity and exhilaration of giving birth naturally, along with its many physical advantages, which lead us to the next most important thing to know: **Natural delivery is usually the ideal method of childbirth.**

There are as many labor and delivery stories as there are babies. No two experiences of labor are exactly the same. Unfortunately, some of the procedures doctors and nurses do during labor to maximize safety and minimize pain reduce chances for a normal delivery. In our efforts to control the whole process, we occasionally cause unnecessary complications. You need to understand what these problems are and how you can best avoid them.

The Natural Course of Labor

During a natural, spontaneous labor, contractions begin with gradually increasing strength and frequency. These contractions eventually thin and dilate the cervix. As the baby's head presses down into the pelvis, the cervix retracts around it.

During labor, the membranes around the baby spontaneously rupture, and some amniotic fluid leaks out. The timing of this event varies greatly.

The baby's head is flexed with his chin on his chest. As the head reaches the last few centimeters of pelvic space, it presses on your rectum, and you will feel an intense urge to bear down. The combination of uterine contractions and maternal pushing efforts forces the baby's head to stretch out the muscles of the lower pelvis, the perineum, and the vaginal opening.

The baby's head now straightens, further opening the vagina (see figure 4). As the baby's head slowly slides through the opening, there may be some tears in the maternal skin or lining of the vagina. This is more common during a first delivery. After the head is out, the rest of the body follows rather quickly. During the next 20 or 30 minutes, the placenta is spontaneously expelled from the uterus and vagina.

Figure 4
Delivery of Baby's Head

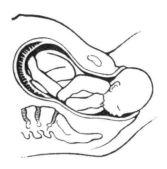

The duration of this entire process varies tremendously. Certainly, it is longer for a first delivery than for following deliveries. The pushing stage of a first labor averages 51 minutes, and for a second baby, 17 minutes.

When to Come to the Hospital

If this is your first baby and your pregnancy has been uncomplicated, it is generally best to stay at home when you are in early labor. Why? Because tension and anxiety in labor leads to unnecessarily long labors, with significantly increased risks of cesareans, Pitocin drips, and forceps deliveries.

A hospital is a tense place. Even if you are visiting someone else, who is a patient there, you feel tense just stepping into the building. When you are the patient, that anxiety increases dramatically.

For the laboring woman who comes to the hospital, the routine practices of fetal monitoring, intravenous (IV) infusions, hospital gowns, blood tests, confinement to a bed, pelvic exams, and blood pressure checks all increase anxiety.

Keep in mind that the average first labor usually lasts eleven hours, so you have lots of time. Under most circumstances, women having their first baby can wait until their contractions are very intense and three to four minutes apart for two hours before going to the hospital.

Very intense. What does that mean? If, during a contraction, you can walk or carry on a conversation, it is not intense enough to start your two-hour clock. If, however, you are finding yourself subconsciously gripping onto the furniture or breathing through your teeth, that's intense. It is at this time that you <u>start</u> your two-hour clock. During that time, you can take a long, warm bath, get your hospital bag together, drink lots of clear fluids, and try to stay calm. Do not eat solid foods.

At the end of these two hours, call the nurses in the Labor and Delivery Unit at your hospital and let them know that you are coming in.

If, at any time, you experience a gush of water coming out of your vagina or start bleeding like a period or heavier, do not wait those two hours. Just call and go in.

Do not try to drive yourself in. Be sure to tell the driver not to race to the hospital. Most hospitals suggest that laboring mothers go first to the Emergency Ward entrance. However, you should clarify where you should go before you leave home.

Our experience with first-time mothers who follow this advice has been excellent. Generally, they arrive with their cervix dilated four to six centimeters and are well into the labor process. If you follow this advice, you will never be sent home in false labor.

If you have had labor before, or had some problems in your pregnancy that may require an early labor evaluation (e.g. previous cesarean, poor fetal growth, high blood pressure), you will need advice from your doctor or midwife on how long to wait before coming in.

During Labor

Typical hospital treatment of healthy, normal laboring women is often unintentionally unkind. They are not allowed to eat anything. They have IV needles stuck in an arm or hand and are practically immobilized by fetal monitors. If they are really unlucky, they suffer through the aggravations and indignities of a perineal shave and an enema. For most women, very little of this abuse is necessary when the labor process is going smoothly, and we are going to help you avoid it.

Diet in Labor

It is not unusual for a laboring woman to vomit sometime during labor. If you were to inhale partially digested food into your lungs, you could get very sick. This is the main reason we suggest not eating solid food when you are in labor.

What about liquids? Labor is hard work, and much bodily fluid is lost and needs replacing during those hours. Well-hydrated women have faster labors than those who are poorly hydrated. You should drink a lot of clear fluids in early labor.

Intravenous Fluids

For some laboring women, IV fluids are very important. There are many circumstances where rapid hydration is critical. With an IV in place, medicines can be introduced into the bloodstream slowly or quickly to solve a variety of problems.

For women having a second, third, or fourth baby, IVs are usually unnecessary. However, practically every labor and delivery unit in the United States will automatically insist that all of their laboring women have one. If you have had a previously uncomplicated delivery, you can request that no IV be started unless it is needed. This, too, should be discussed with your obstetrician in advance. He may have a good reason for you to have an IV. If so, he should let you know what it is.

If this is your first labor, an IV is usually, but not always, a good idea. First labors are usually longer and more difficult, so IV hydration and medications are frequently needed.

Enemas and Shaves

Not too many years ago, standard procedure was for the obstetric nurse to shave the laboring woman's perineal hair and give her an enema to clear the rectum of stool. Few hospitals do this routinely anymore. There is no advantage to these procedures, and they are debasing. Even if your hospital routinely does this to laboring women, you do not have to agree to have it done to you. You always have the right to say "NO".

To avoid unnecessary procedures

- By 32 to 36 weeks, find out what labor and delivery procedures are routine in your hospital.
- Discuss with your doctor any procedures you find objectionable.
- Ask for your requests to be written on the front of the prenatal record or birth plan.
- If, when you are in labor, your requests are ignored, remember that you are in control. You have the right to refuse any and all procedures you feel are unnecessary and annoying.

Uterine and Fetal Monitors

Technology and nature are not usually compatible. This is particularly true in the case of fetal monitoring and labor.

Continuous fetal heart-rate monitoring usually requires a pregnant woman to wear at least one belt across her uterus, which may or may not be uncomfortable during labor (see figure 5). In any case, it requires you to be relatively immobile and is a distraction at a time when you do not need additional aggravation. Often, a small wire called a fetal scalp electrode is inserted through the vagina and placed on the baby's head for more accurate tracings. This may allow elimination of one of the belts. Another belt, which monitors contractions, may be taken off if an intrauterine pressure catheter is placed inside your uterus alongside the baby. The technology is terrific, but all these things that we do to you may be rather annoying and overly aggressive when you are in labor.

Figure 5
Fetal and Uterine Monitors

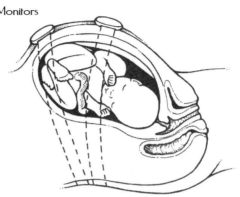

Another method of fetal evaluation is simply listening to the baby's heart rate (auscultation) every 15 to 30 minutes in the first stage of labor with a special stethoscope, and more frequently in the second stage when you are pushing. This is a lot less annoying for you and probably just as accurate in determining fetal heart-rate evidence of true fetal distress. Unfortunately, it is more time consuming for the nurses and does not supply doctors with the kind of data which may be helpful in a malpractice case. Because of that, most American women are placed on the fetal monitor continuously throughout their labor.

It is true that, on rare occasions, a baby's life will be saved or dramatically improved because of knowledge obtained by the fetal monitor, however, it is also true that at least 99 percent of babies receive no benefit from being monitored continuously. Unfortunately, many thousands of American women undergo unnecessary emergency cesarean sections because of an erroneous diagnosis of "fetal distress."

An additional unexpected psychological problem with fetal monitors is that, by their very nature, they tend to increase tension in the nurses and doctors. This leads to increased tension for the laboring woman, which then often translates into an increase in the sensation of pain in labor.

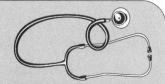

From the Doctor's Files

I have used fetal monitors for more than 30 years on thousands of pregnant women. My impression is that it is best to avoid continuous electronic monitoring in labor if mother and baby have no significant risk factors.

Most serious problems identifiable by the fetal monitor are found in the first few minutes of monitoring. Therefore after an initial 15-20 minutes on the electronic fetal monitor, you can insist on evaluation by auscultation alone, unless you have some very specific factors which place your baby at a higher risk for problems. Discuss this with your doctor or midwife well before you go into labor. If you can avoid the fetal monitor for most of your labor, your chances of unnecessary poking, prodding, and pain decrease.

Mobility

If you are having a normal, uncomplicated labor and want to walk around or sit up in a chair, you should do so unless there are compelling reasons not to. In fact, women who are up and about tend to have shorter labors than those who are in bed. Your hospital may have devices, called telemetry devices, which monitor the baby's heartbeat and your contractions and yet allow you to walk around. This is much better than being stuck in a bed. You can ask for these devices if you must have electronic monitoring. If you have a monitor on, you can ask to have it removed. If the nurse doesn't want to remove it, and it is bothering you, you can remove it yourself.

There are exceptions to this recommendation. Women who already have an epidural anesthetic in place, have just received narcotics, or are having a medically complicated pregnancy would be wise to keep the monitor on.

Episiotomy

An episiotomy is an intentional surgical cut made at the most posterior part of the vagina as the baby's head is coming out. The purpose is to allow more room for the head and possibly to speed up the delivery process. These are only done with adequate anesthesia, so you should not feel it.

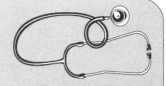

From the Nurse's Notes

There are two types of episiotomies—midline and mediolateral (see figure 6). Generally speaking, doctors are more likely to do episiotomies than midwives. Most episiotomies can be avoided with patience and perineal massage—something midwives are more comfortable with.

Mediolateral episiotomies are generally far more painful than the more standard midline episiotomy, and it is not uncommon for women to have painful intercourse for months afterwards. Ask your doctor what kind of episiotomy he usually makes. If he says mediolateral, talk him out of it. That is not something you will need to have done to you, except in rare circumstances.

Figure 6
Episiotomies

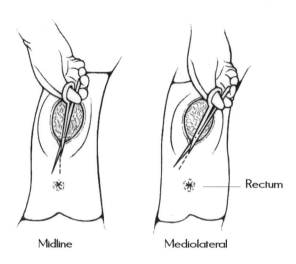

Midline   Mediolateral   Rectum

You should also discuss whether or not you will even need an episiotomy at all. Your doctor will often bend to your wishes if you state them clearly. This is best done weeks before you go into labor.

Forceps and Vacuum Deliveries

Most babies can deliver safely without any special help. Occasionally, however, a baby's head gets stuck in his mother's pelvis and some kind of instrument is needed to pull him through. The tools we have available for this purpose are obstetric forceps and vacuum extractors (see figure 7). **When properly used, they are safe, time-saving, and potentially life-saving instruments. Improperly used, they can be dangerous.**

Obstetric forceps are metal instruments of varying length, usually about a foot and a half long with flattened spoon-like ends that slide over the side of the baby's head. After placing the forceps on each side of the baby's head, the obstetrician can then pull the baby out.

Figure 7
Applications

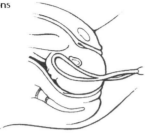
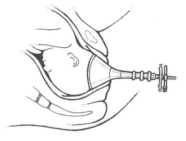

Forceps Application   Vacuum Application

Most pregnant women shudder at the thought of their baby being delivered by forceps. They have heard stories of severely injured and brain damaged babies and lacerated mothers. They want to avoid forceps deliveries at all cost. Unfortunately, they haven't heard of the many millions of healthy American children and adults who have been safely delivered by the use of forceps.

Vacuum extractors use a suction device (usually plastic) attached to a handle. The suction cup is placed on the top of the baby's head and the doctor then pulls the baby out. Visually, the vacuum extractor looks a lot safer than forceps, but it, too, has a small, but real, possibility for injury to both mother and baby.

If used under the right conditions, either device is safe and effective. But if used when the baby's head is too high, too much effort is applied, or if improperly placed, either device may cause injury.

In general, because of the safety concerns of instrument delivery, it is best to try to avoid those circumstances which lead to their use. By far, the most common reason for instrument deliveries is the lack of effective maternal pushing efforts with epidural anesthesia, primarily with first babies.

Pushing a first baby out is hard work, requiring strong muscles, time, and an intense need to bear down. Epidural anesthesia, while wonderful for pain relief, usually diminishes muscle power and inhibits the bearing down instinct so critical for a natural delivery.

The other factor, time, is also important. Under natural circumstances, we usually use two hours as a relative time limit for the second stage of labor (pushing). If a baby hasn't come out (or isn't close to coming out) after two hours, this usually indicates a problem, and obstetricians begin to devise solutions, e.g., cesarean section, instrument delivery, medicine (Pitocin) to strengthen contractions, or simply allowing more time.

When epidural anesthesia is used, this two-hour limit is much too short. For a first baby, it may take three to four hours to push him out.

Avoiding an instrument delivery

- Tell your doctor if you want to avoid instrument delivery long before you go into labor. Have it written on the front of your prenatal record.
- Try to avoid getting epidural anesthesia.
- Keep in mind that the longer and harder you push, the higher your chances are for a natural delivery.
- Wait to begin pushing until you feel an urge to do so. Pushing before you feel this urge is seldom helpful and may wear you out unnecessarily.
- When pushing hurts, don't back off. When it hurts the most, push the hardest, and you'll get done a lot quicker. This concept is by far the most important for effective pushing, but also the hardest to actually do.
- When pushing, forget about good manners. If you try to hold back urine or stool when pushing, you will hold the baby back too. Push everything out.
- Begin early in your pregnancy to make a serious dietary effort to keep your baby from being unnecessarily large at delivery. Minimize your sugar intake.

If you decide on an epidural and want to avoid instrument delivery or cesarean section, in addition to the above suggestions, give yourself a lot of extra time to push the baby out. If you are relatively comfortable, the fetal heart tones are reassuring and you are making slow, but steady, progress in pushing the baby's head down, there really is no particular time limit for your baby to be born.

Vaginal delivery of a second baby is very different than that of a first baby in that it requires far less pushing to stretch out the vaginal tissues. Epidural anesthesia for a second delivery is probably not going to dramatically increase the risk of an instrument delivery or cesarean section. More than 90% of instrument deliveries are for first babies. This general subject is a good thing to discuss with your doctor early on in the pregnancy. Some doctors are very aggressive with the use of forceps or vacuum delivery and will tell you that you have nothing to worry about. Other physicians will be more than happy to accede to your wishes if you want to try to avoid instrument deliveries.

In some places in this country, up to 40 percent of vaginal deliveries are done with forceps or vacuum. This is way too high. In our institution, for the past 15,000 deliveries, our instrument delivery rate has been less than 5 percent. It might be helpful for you to know what your hospital's forceps delivery rate is. This information is available to physicians and consumers alike.

Induction of Labor

There are many good medical and obstetric reasons to have your labor started artificially, instead of waiting for it to begin naturally. If your doctor suggests that you or your baby may have a medical problem that should be treated by induction of labor, you would be wise to follow his advice.

Induction of labor may be done in several different ways, and there are advantages and disadvantages to each method.

Rupturing the Membranes

The simplest method is the rupturing of the membranes (ROM), allowing some amniotic fluid to come out of the vagina. This can only be done if the cervix is already open.

Women who are ideal candidates for this type of induction are those whose cervix is already soft, thinning, and two or more centimeters dilated. ROM induction works very well for those women who are near or past their due date and for those who have had babies before.

Usually, women will go into spontaneous labor within a few hours of ROM, and no additional treatment is needed. Sometimes, the results can be surprisingly quick. The shortest time we have seen from ROM without labor to delivery is one hour and 15 minutes. Four to ten hours is the more typical length of time to delivery in women who have had babies before.

This type of induction has the advantage of simplicity and minimal intervention. Labor is otherwise natural, and excessive pain is not present. The disadvantage is that sometimes it doesn't work or is attempted in an inappropriate circumstance. In these cases, effective labor does not occur, and Pitocin induction is then required.

Pitocin Induction

This is the most frequent method of artificially starting labor in the United States. Pitocin is the well-known brand name of a hormone (oxytocin) that causes the uterus to contract. It is very powerful and needs to be given carefully and monitored, so that over-stimulation of the uterus does not occur.

Pitocin is an extremely useful medicine, because it solves so many labor problems. All obstetricians, midwives, and obstetric nurses are very familiar with its use and risks. It is given intravenously, and uterine and fetal monitoring is necessary.

The advantage of Pitocin induction is that it is almost always successful in achieving the goal: labor. The amount of

Pitocin being administered can be adjusted quickly. If your uterus over-responds by contracting too long or too frequently, rapidly decreasing the rate of Pitocin results in a decrease in contractions.

Pitocin induction also has its disadvantages. Most women report that contractions with Pitocin hurt more than natural contractions. The immobility, need for continuous fetal monitoring, and very frequent vital-sign checks are also a big nuisance, but necessary, because if not monitored carefully, Pitocin has the potential to be a dangerous drug.

Prostaglandin Gel Induction

Prostaglandin is a hormone that causes uterine contractions and softens the cervix. This medicine is used primarily to "ripen" the cervix prior to a planned Pitocin induction. Usually, prostaglandin comes in the form of a gel, which is introduced painlessly either in the cervical opening or in the vagina. On occasion, it will actually start labor and may be used for this purpose. The advantage of a prostaglandin induction is the simplicity. The labor that ensues is much like a spontaneous labor in character. IVs and frequent vital-sign checks are not required, although fetal monitoring may be needed because of the possibility of uterine over-stimulation.

The disadvantage is that prostaglandin may not be very effective in initiating labor. It is mostly useful as a pre-induction preparation.

Misoprostol (Cytotec)

Misoprostol is a type of prostaglandin that causes the uterus to contract. In its present FDA-approved use, it relieves the gastrointestinal side effects of medications frequently used by people with arthritis.

It is being used in increasing frequency to induce labor, because it has some remarkable advantages. It is nearly as effective as Pitocin, but much simpler and cheaper.

The procedure is simple: place a pill in the vagina and wait. Under proper circumstances, it works quickly with rare problems of "fetal distress".

What is really phenomenal is the cost differential between one Misoprostol tablet ($1.20) and Pitocin with its associated IV equipment ($97.32). Considering the hundreds of thousands of inductions each year in the United States alone, there is a great potential for significant savings in medical care costs using Misoprostol.

The down side to Misoprostol is that it doesn't always work, so that later in the day, Pitocin may be needed to help achieve effective labor. Also, a small percent of women respond to the medication with too many contractions, requiring another medicine to be used to slow them down.

Elective Induction of Labor

As pregnant women approach their due date, and especially after it comes and goes, there is an increasing desire to go into labor and be done with all the aggravations of late pregnancy.

Most doctors are willing to induce labor after the due date has passed if the woman's cervix is "inducible", i.e., soft, thinning, and open a centimeter or more, with the baby's head relatively low in the pelvis. Inductions with an inducible cervix are almost always successful, resulting in happy mothers and healthy babies.

Advantages of an elective induction

- A family can plan on the timing of labor and adjust family and work schedules accordingly.
- It usually guarantees that the woman's obstetrician will be delivering the baby. That is nice for everyone.
- Induction helps avoid extremely prolonged pregnancies that might otherwise cause problems for babies.
- Inductions reduce maternal anxiety about having enough time to get to the hospital. This is especially true in rural areas.

Unfortunately, not all elective inductions turn out well, usually because they are started when the cervix is not inducible. Trying to induce labor when the cervix is closed, long, and firm frequently leads to failure, resulting in long, exhausting labors and many unnecessary cesarean sections, infections, and hemorrhages.

When a woman's cervix is not inducible, it is generally wiser to be a little more patient. This is often frustrating, but waiting until there are cervical changes will allow for a higher likelihood of a normal labor and delivery.

Cesarean Sections

A cesarean section (or perhaps known also by its more politically correct term, cesarean delivery) is an abdominal operation, requiring incisions through the skin and uterus to deliver the baby.

The vast majority of women who have this procedure recover well, without medical complications, and are well enough to go home three days after surgery. Medication is available which reduces, but does not eliminate, the post-operative pain.

Total recovery time from the physical effects of these operations varies from person to person, but most women are back to normal activity about two weeks after returning home.

A woman who has had a cesarean section can safely breastfeed despite the pain medicines, so having a cesarean section should not keep women from nursing.

Being home with a new baby in the first two weeks after having had a cesarean is much more difficult than after having had a vaginal delivery. Typically, at a time when she wants to be doing many things with her baby, the new mother is doing well just to take care of herself. It is a tiring time under normal circumstances, and much more so if the woman is recovering from major surgery.

Surgical Risks

Every operation has it risks. This is true of heart transplants, cesarean sections, and mole removals alike. Most of the time, as patients, we accept these risks because the potential good of the operation far outweighs the potential complications. In our modern, high-tech medical institutions, we expect great things to happen, and, for the most part, they do. Physicians and consumers alike tend to get complacent about surgical risks for those relatively low risk operations such as appendectomies, scheduled repeat cesarean sections, hysterectomies, and the like. However, bad things can, and do, happen unexpectedly during surgery or after.

We usually think of postoperative complications as those which happen within the first few days of surgery. These are certainly the most common and obvious: infection, bleeding, incisional problems, etc. But there are postoperative problems which may not occur for years.

This problem of long-delayed postoperative complications is especially true in obstetrical care. Since 1990, nearly one in every four American pregnant women has had her baby delivered by cesarean section. This high cesarean section rate has resulted in millions of women facing a next pregnancy with a scarred uterus that has the potential for rupturing in labor leading to catastrophe for both mother and baby. One result of having a cesarean is that, in a following pregnancy, about 70-75 percent of these women will have a repeated cesarean, with all of the associated risks of major surgery.

Minimizing your Chances for a Cesarean

There are many serious problems in pregnancy that clearly are best handled by a cesarean section. There is usually little you or your doctor can do to avoid them. These include: placenta previa (placenta is coming first), heavy vaginal bleeding from placental separation, abnormal positions of the baby, true "fetal distress", prolonged hard labor without progress, and a variety of others.

Many other situations leading to cesareans can be avoided. You have some control over these situations.

How to avoid an unnecessary cesarean

- Avoid unnecessary inductions of labor.
- Go to a midwife for prenatal care.
- Find a doctor with a low cesarean section rate and tell him you want to avoid a cesarean.
- Avoid excessive maternal and fetal weight gain by limiting your sugar intake throughout your pregnancy (See Appendix II).
- Begin a muscle relaxation program by mid-pregnancy and use it when you are in labor (See Appendix I).
- Avoid epidural anesthesia, if possible, for your first baby.
- Use effective pushing techniques in the second stage of labor.
- Unless medically indicated, avoid continuous electronic fetal monitors when you are in labor.

- Drink a lot of fluids when you are in labor.
- Have someone you know and trust with you throughout the active part of your labor.
- Be patient if you are having a slow labor.
- Unless you have diabetes, avoid an ultrasound late in pregnancy if the baby seems big (see chapter 8).
- Consider external version or vaginal delivery for breech babies.
- If you have had a cesarean before, consider a trial of labor this time.

Vaginal Birth After Cesarean (VBAC)

From the early 1900's until the 1980's, if an American woman had a cesarean section in one pregnancy, she was destined to have a cesarean section for all future deliveries. The dictum "once a cesarean, always a cesarean" was taken very seriously by American obstetricians.

From the Doctor's Files

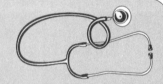

In 1974, I was in my second year of my obstetric residency, and, as most residents do, I was voraciously reading all I could about obstetrical care. I came upon some European literature, suggesting that VBACs were safe to do. So, when an appropriate pregnant candidate showed up in labor, we discussed VBAC, and she was all for it. She proceeded to have a nice, normal vaginal delivery of a healthy baby and was delighted to have avoided the scalpel.

The next day, the attending staff doctor—my boss—found out about the delivery and was livid. To say he reamed me out would be a gross understatement. I was in hot water for not following "The Dictum," even though everything turned out very well for mother and baby. Fortunately, time cools hot water, and my residency went on uninterrupted by this heinous crime.

In the past 25 years, there has been a turn in favor of allowing labor to occur, since most of these women can deliver normally. Several large American studies have shown that this is a reasonably safe thing to do, and, if given the opportunity, about 70 - 80 percent of women with a previous cesarean section who go into labor could deliver vaginally. There is about a 0.5 percent risk of uterine rupture after spontaneous labor and about 0.2 percent chance of serious harm to the baby. These risks are higher if labor is induced. Nonetheless, only about one in four American women with previous cesareans have VBACs.

Most women who have had previous cesareans can safely have a trial of labor with their next pregnancies. The chance of success is high and the risks are very low. There are, however, some uncontrollable circumstances which do suggest having a repeat cesarean, such as a previous vertical (up and down) or classical (high vertical) incision in the uterus, a very small maternal pelvis, more than two previous cesareans, or a previous failed trial of labor after a previous cesarean section.

Barriers of the Medical System

Many doctors who deliver in small rural hospitals are very uncomfortable with the concept of trial of labor after a previous cesarean section, because they may not have readily available surgeons and surgical teams to do a rapid cesarean section if one is needed. Instead of suggesting that the pregnant woman go to a larger hospital for a VBAC, he may just insist on scheduling a repeat cesarean section. This is more beneficial to him than to his pregnant patient.

A trial of labor after a previous cesarean, even in a larger hospital with surgical and anesthesia staff available at all times, carries a small, but real risk of needing an emergency cesarean in the case of a rupturing uterus. It also requires that the physician be immediately available during the labor. This often does not set well with a lot of doctors, who also have office responsibilities. For this reason alone, many doctors do not encourage VBACs to their patients, who would otherwise benefit from avoiding a cesarean.

If you have had a previous cesarean section for a non-repeatable cause, such as "fetal distress", breech presentation, placenta previa, etc., it is usually in your best interest to plan on a VBAC. If your present doctor does not agree with you, find out why. If he has no strong reason and you can't change his mind, get a second opinion from another doctor. There are plenty of doctors who strongly encourage VBACs.

Sometimes, the barrier to avoiding a repeat cesarean section is the medical circumstance. Sometimes, it is the obstetrician who discourages a VBAC for his own personal time-management concerns. Quite often, however, it is the woman herself who is the main barrier to her own best obstetric care.

Fear of labor, fear of vaginal delivery, fear of going through labor only to have a cesarean, fear of again experiencing the stress of "fetal distress" in labor, fear of failure, fear of a ruptured uterus, fear of any or all of these things causes many women to refuse to go through labor and insist on an elective repeat cesarean section. In spite of the overwhelming evidence that a repeat cesarean section is more dangerous for them than a normal delivery, and in spite of their doctors' encouragement for a VBAC, they insist on avoiding a trial of labor.

There are some of you who have gone through a long labor only to end up with a cesarean section for failing to progress toward delivery. The prospect of another exhausting and fruitless labor like that is not very appealing. This is very understandable, but take heart. About 50-60 percent of women in your situation successfully deliver vaginally the next time. This number is even higher for those who, in early pregnancy, get instructed on a diabetic diet to keep their babies from getting unnecessarily big and fat and hard to deliver. In our experience, about 90 percent of these women safely deliver vaginally, and 95 percent have smaller babies than they had previously. These babies have been as healthy as their older siblings.

From the Doctor's Files

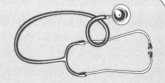

Sometimes, failure to progress in a first labor has more to do with the quality of the uterine contractions than the size of the baby. Several years ago, I took care of a woman who had previously had a cesarean for failing to progress in labor with a 7-pound, 8-ounce baby. I encouraged her to think positively about a VBAC this time. She did so and went into labor on her own at term. She had a normal labor and delivered a 10-pound, 4-ounce baby vaginally, and both of them did very well. The size of this baby surprised us both. Had I known the size of the baby before labor, I might not have suggested that she try for a VBAC. In this case, ignorance was bliss.

Before You Have a Cesarean

Most often, the decision to have a cesarean is made while a woman is in labor, when anxiety levels are high. Mothers do not think to ask all the right questions at these times. Even more significant, this is a time of severe dependency, and the woman in painful labor usually abrogates all of her responsibility and lets the doctor do whatever he thinks is best. It is not generally a good time to talk about two very important aspects of a cesarean: anesthesia and the type of incision. These are topics to discuss weeks before your due date, and have written on the front of the prenatal chart.

Type of Incision

There are two types of skin incisions for cesarean sections: vertical (up and down) and horizontal ("bikini cut"), also called a Pfannenstiel incision (see figure 8). Nearly all physicians doing cesarean sections are capable of doing either type of incision. However, some physicians do not like to do the bikini cut because it takes a little more time, and is somewhat more difficult to do.

For most babies requiring a cesarean section for entry into the world, the type of skin incision is immaterial, because they can fit through either one. However, for you, the person who will be recovering from the surgery and looking at your belly for another fifty years or so, the difference in skin incisions can be major.

The bikini cut scar is by far better looking. It is made across the top of the pubic hair line (after the hair is shaved off) and may be from four to six inches long. The scar, six months later, is often hard to see, as it is covered either with hair, underwear, or the lower half of a bikini swimsuit.

Figure 8
Cesarean Section Incision Sites

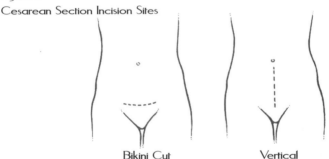

Bikini Cut   Vertical

The up and down incision not only leaves an ugly, unwanted scar, but is associated with more pain and problems. About 95 percent of cesarean sections can be done with bikini cuts. They can be done even when a woman has had a previous up and down incision, and the postoperative recovery is so much easier.

There are some occasions where an up and down incision is a much better choice, such as in the case of triplets (or more), fetal hydrocephalus (the baby has a very large head), a serious bleeding problem known as DIC (disseminated intravascular coagulopathy), etc. These problems occur very infrequently.

From the Doctor's Files

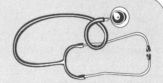

Most doctors feel that they can get a baby out faster in an emergency through an up and down incision. However, because I do so many bikini cut incisions, I even do emergency cesareans this way, and so do many other doctors. You can request this incision even in an emergency situation.

Some doctors will automatically do an up and down incision for cesarean sections, unless specifically told to do a bikini cut. Be sure that you discuss this with your doctor before any decisions are made, or else you may be looking at a nasty scar for the rest of your life.

Chapter 7

Breastfeeding

During your pregnancy you will want to make the best decisions you can about the health of your baby. The decision which has the most impact on your baby's health is one over which you have complete control: Whether to breast or bottle feed.

Therefore it is vital that you know that **breastfeeding is significantly healthier for your baby than bottle-feeding.**

Until recently, the benefits of breastfeeding have been undervalued, while companies producing infant formulas have been very successful in their efforts to get mothers to bottle feed their babies.

There is now a major movement underway to help mothers decide to breastfeed. It's about time. The American Academy of Pediatrics, the American College of Obstetrics and Gynecology, the American College of Nurse-Midwives, the World Health Organization, and UNICEF are just a few of the health organizations rallying to promote breastfeeding.

In spite of what you may read or hear from friends or formula companies, the nutritional value and health benefits of artificially produced infant formulas are not equal to that of breast milk. Breast milk is better. It always has been, and always will be.

From the Nurse's Notes

Saying to yourself, "I am making the best decision for my baby, myself, my family, community, and the world" is very empowering.

History and Trends

Trends are ever-changing when it comes to feeding infants. It is most likely that your mother breastfed, your grandmother did not, and your great-grandmother may have even used a wet-nurse. Wet-nurses were women hired to breastfeed babies of other women.

In the days before the invention of a safe mass-produced infant formula, many babies survived only because they lived on the breast milk of their wet-nurses. Feeding a baby with inadequate formula (called "dry-nursing") almost always ended in the infant's death.

Wet-nursing dates back to biblical times. Moses was breastfed by a wet-nurse, which saved his life. The four wives of Jacob breastfed one another's children. The pharaohs of Egypt used wet-nurses. The Romans and Greeks hired slaves to nurse their babies. If a woman nursed several unrelated babies, these babies were considered milk brothers or sisters, and were prevented from inter-marrying.

Throughout history, many poor women became pregnant solely to be able to earn money by breastfeeding the children of other women.

If you would like to know more about the history and profession of wet-nurses, read an enlightening book by Naimi Baumslag and Dia L. Michels called <u>Milk, Money, and Madness.</u>

Benefits to Baby

Breast milk is quite simply a baby's perfect food. It is species-specific, meaning that it is made specifically for your baby's digestive system. Because your baby digests it so easily, feeding problems, diarrhea, gas pains, and constipation are minimized. The protein and fat in breast milk are made for the newborn's body and are more easily and completely absorbed than that of infant formulas. Breast milk is custom-made, nutritionally complete, and, of course, free.

In their first year, breastfed babies have fewer medical problems compared to formula-fed babies. Specifically, they have a lower incidence of ear infections, diarrhea, bacterial infections, respiratory illnesses, and sudden infant death syndrome (SIDS). This translates to a healthier, happier baby (and mother), and fewer trips to doctors and emergency wards.

As they grow older, breastfed babies have decreased chances of developing diabetes (types 1 and 2), inflammatory bowel diseases, lymphoma, allergic disorders, and a variety of other chronic digestive disorders.

Future tooth decay, distortion of facial muscles, and malocclusion (improper meeting of upper and lower teeth) may all result directly from sucking on rubber nipples and pacifiers. If you choose to breastfeed, your child's future dental bills will thus be lower.

Human breast milk contains high concentrations of an important fatty acid called docosahexaenoic acid (DHA). DHA is critical for brain growth and development. The human brain triples in size during infancy and is 90 percent of adult size by age two. Until recently, infant formulas did not contain DHA. Now (at an additional price) some formulas will contain this very important ingredient. The DHA in breast milk is free.

Children who are breastfed are less likely to become obese. In our society, obese children and adults not only suffer from poor physical health, they also have to deal with a lack of acceptance, which often leads to poor mental health.

How can we put a price tag on all these benefits?

For premature babies, breast milk provides protection against complications from the life-threatening diseases of necrotizing enterocolitis and bacterial sepsis. The medical staff at most intensive care nurseries strongly encourage breastfeeding and offer technical assistance, which allows even the smallest premature baby the opportunity to get the benefits of breast milk.

Benefits to Mother

Your baby isn't the only benefactor from breastfeeding. Mothers benefit in many ways also.

Breastfeeding increases the production of a hormone called Oxytocin. Oxytocin causes the uterus to contract and shrink, resulting in less blood loss after delivery. Another hormone, Prolactin, is increased, and has a tranquilizing effect, which allows for better sleep. Some studies show that breastfeeding mothers return to their pre-pregnancy weight more quickly than those who formula feed. Maintaining this weight is more likely with six months or more of breastfeeding.

Breastfeeding also acts as nature's birth control. Studies show that mothers who breastfeed at least three to four times per day will not ovulate before eight weeks postpartum. Also, women who breastfeed exclusively (no formula at all) for the first six months have only a 1 percent chance of pregnancy, which is about the same as taking birth control pills.

After the first six months, the chance for pregnancy gradually increases and breastfeeding is not a generally reliable method of birth control. However, there are many women who do not ovulate for 1 1/2 to 2 years while they are breastfeeding.

The medical benefits for mothers who breastfeed go far beyond the first year after delivery. Diseases which have been shown to be reduced in women who breastfeed their babies include: breast cancer, ovarian cancer, uterine cancer, heart disease, osteoporosis, and diabetes (type 2).

All the maternal benefits listed above have been proven scientifically. It is difficult to prove that maternal-infant bonding increases with breastfeeding, but there is a great deal of evidence supporting the concept that both mothers and babies benefit psychologically with breastfeeding.

From the Nurse's Notes

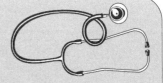

In retrospect, I would gladly have given over the labor experience to my husband, but never would I have relinquished breast-feeding.

Benefits to other Family Members

A major benefit is that you will have more money. Because of fewer episodes of infant illness, parents have less time absent from work. The cost of purchasing formula for the first year of a baby's life is $1,000 to $1,500. Since breastfed babies are healthier, less money (and time) will be spent at the doctor's office.

For infants, three months of breastfeeding has been shown to reduce health care costs by as much as $475. (1999 figures)

Environmental and Societal Benefits

It is empowering to have a positive impact on the world around us. The environmental cost of bottles, nipples, boxes, advertising, and the production and transportation of formula for millions of American babies every year is staggering.

Employer Benefits

You might think that your employer will not want to hire or retain breastfeeding mothers. Maybe so. However, the thoughtful employer, and there are many, will realize that breastfeeding leads to lower staff turnover, less sick time, lower health care costs, and increased job satisfaction and productivity. Employers who encourage breastfeeding have recruitment incentives for women and develop a reputation as caring for their employees' family welfare.

Barriers to Breastfeeding

Perhaps unknowingly, your doctor's office and the hospital where you deliver your baby may play a big role in discouraging successful breastfeeding.

Infant formula companies have been very successful in promoting their product. In most American hospitals, they provide infant formula to newborn nurseries either free of charge or for a very low cost. This saves hospitals many thousands of dollars each year. In addition, each new mother gets a gift pack, which includes a supply of formula and bottles to feed their babies.

Your doctor's office probably has promotional material encouraging formula-feeding and very little, if any, information on breastfeeding. The magazines in the waiting room, in addition to basic parenting tips, contain page after page of advertisements and promotions for infant formula.

The formula companies do all this because it works to increase bottle-feeding and thereby reduce breastfeeding. It effectively increases the sales of their products. In essence, those doctor's offices and hospitals are acting as salesmen for infant formula!

> Formula advertising significantly reduces breastfeeding success in the first two weeks after delivery. **Formula promotion products should be eliminated from prenatal settings.**

When you and your baby are in the hospital, standard nursery policies and activities may also inadvertently become barriers to successful breastfeeding. Practices such as separation of the baby from the mother during the immediate recovery period, postponing the first breastfeeding, discouraging rooming-in, giving the baby supplements, and very early discharge from the hospital, while possibly well-meaning and entrenched in hospital policy, subtly but effectively reduce the number of successfully breastfed babies.

Other societal barriers are less obvious and therefore more difficult to overcome. Employers who do not provide private areas for mothers to breastfeed their babies are barriers. Grandmothers who discourage breastfeeding have a powerful negative influence. A general societal aversion to having mothers breastfeed publicly can put a great deal of strain on breastfeeding mothers. These are purely cultural phenomena.

> In Sweden, it is considered unethical to artificially feed your baby.

Is Breastfeeding for Everyone?

No. There are certain medical conditions, which will prevent breastfeeding. Mothers who have contagious diseases such as the human immunodeficiency virus (HIV), viral hepatitis, active untreated tuberculosis, and whooping cough may pass these diseases to the baby in the breast milk and therefore should not breastfeed.

Women who use illegal drugs or are heavy alcohol drinkers are advised not to breastfeed.

While taking the following medications, women should abstain from breastfeeding: Amethopterin, Chloramphenicol, Cimetidine, Clemastine, Cyclophosphamide, Ergotamine, GoldSalts, Methimazole, Methotrexate, Metronidazole, Phenindione, Thiouracil. The radioactive drugs Gallium-69, Iodine-125, Iodine-131, Radioactive Sodium, and Technetium-99m are also contraindicated.

Women who have had breast reduction surgery may still be able to nurse if milk ducts and nerves were not severed. If they were, breast-feeding can lead to some very painful consequences. Check with your breast surgeon if you have had this procedure.

Implant surgery to enhance breast size should not interfere with the ability to breastfeed successfully. Women undergoing breast cancer treatment, however, cannot breastfeed.

Nearly all over-the-counter medications can be safely taken by breastfeeding mothers (see Chapter 3). However, according to Dr. Ruth A. Lawrence, pediatrician and lactation specialist, certain over-the-counter herbal medicines may not be safe. These include: Fenugreek (also called Greek Hayseed), Comfrey, Gingko, Fennel, Echinacea, and Ginseng. The following herbal teas are considered safe: Chicory, Orange Spice, Peppermint, Raspberry, Red Bush, and Rose Hips.

Overcoming the Barriers

For decades, The American Academy of Pediatrics (AAP), the professional organization of pediatricians, has been concerned about setting guidelines for proper nutrition for infants and children. In 1948 the AAP recommended that every effort be made to have new mothers breastfeed their full-term infants. Since then, there have been considerable advances in the scientific knowledge of breastfeeding and the mechanisms of its beneficial effects. This understanding has compelled the AAP to issue a new strong statement,(See Appendix III) promoting breast-feeding for all infants, ideally up to 12 months. We applaud the AAP for this action.

AAP Recommended Breastfeeding Practices

- Breast milk is preferred over artificial milk.
- Breastfeeding should begin within the first hour after birth.
- Newborns should be nursed whenever they show signs of hunger.
- No supplements should be given.
- Infants should be assessed by five to seven days of age.
- Exclusive breastfeeding is ideal and sufficient nutrition for the first six months of life.
- Every effort should be made to maintain breastfeeding if mother is hospitalized.

The United States Department of Health and Human Services has stated that breastfeeding is one of the most important contributors to infant health. In 2001 it prepared its Blueprint for Action on Breastfeeding which was widely distributed to physicians and medical organizations. This plan recommends a variety of community programs whose goal is "to shape a future in which mothers can feel comfortable and free to breastfeed their children without societal hindrances".

In addition to the these efforts, the World Health Organization (WHO) and UNICEF in 1991 launched a baby-friendly hospital initiative whose aim is to give every baby the best start in life, by ensuring a health care setting where breastfeeding is the norm.

Hospitals throughout the world can become officially designated as "Baby Friendly" if they meet certain strict criteria and standards. Achieving this official designation has become a symbol of great pride for 14,000 hospitals worldwide and is a highly coveted award. Many hospitals are presently changing their policies in an attempt to become labeled Baby Friendly.

The most difficult change hospitals must make is no longer accepting free formula and paying a fair market price for the formula they use in their nurseries. **Accepting free formula is an unethical barrier to breastfeeding.**

Baby Friendly hospitals must discontinue sending new mothers home with gift packs from formula companies, and a wide variety of postpartum and nursery practices need to be changed to enhance and promote successful breastfeeding.

If you are lucky, you will have a hospital in your community which has achieved a Baby Friendly designation, or is actively working toward that goal.

> To request the list of United States hospitals that have received the Baby Friendly designation, contact: Baby-Friendly USA, 8 Sebastian Way #13, Sandwich MA 02563. Telephone # (508) 888-8044.

If your hospital does not fit this description, you can help to stimulate a positive change by discussing this with your obstetrician, his nurse, and the nurses who work in the postpartum area or newborn nursery. Better yet, write a letter to your hospital administrator, requesting the hospital make the commitment to become designated as "Baby Friendly."

Tips for Successful Breastfeeding

Your breasts have a purpose. They are milk-secreting glands. It is plain and simple; the milk they secrete provides all the nutrients your healthy infant needs until six months of age.

Is breastfeeding natural? Absolutely.

Is breastfeeding easy? No, not necessarily. It takes commitment and dedication. Early in your pregnancy, you might want to develop a strategy or plan to help overcome any difficulties that may come with breastfeeding. Resources are abundant, but it certainly will help if you are aware of them beforehand. A little preparation will help you choose breastfeeding and continue successfully.

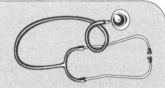

From the Nurse's Notes

For Successful Breastfeeding Initiation:
1. Begin breastfeeding soon after delivery, usually within the first hour.
2. Keep your baby in your hospital room with you if at all possible.
3. Feed your baby when he shows signs of hunger, such as increased alertness or activity, mouthing or rooting. Crying is a late sign of hunger.
4. Nurse your baby 8 to 12 times every 24 hours, or 10 to 15 minutes on each breast. Non-demanding babies should be aroused to feed if four hours have passed since the last feeding.
5. Take advantage of the advice of a lactation specialist. Most large hospitals have one.
6. For the first week or two, keep a journal of each feeding, urination and stool. Bring this journal to the first baby appointment. It will help you evaluate your success with breastfeeding.
7. Do not give your baby supplements unless medically necessary. Pacifiers should be withheld until breastfeeding is well established.
8. Drink lots of fluids. Do not let yourself get dehydrated.
    There may be times when you will need to use a breast

pump to get milk from your breast to a bottle for later use. Breast pumps can be very simple and mechanical or some- what elaborate and electrical. They do not hurt. Initially, breast pumps are commonly used when the baby is prema- ture or needs special medical attention in the hospital. Later on, breast pumping may be helpful to store breast milk for more convenient timing of feeding.

Support Groups

During your pregnancy you can obtain excellent informa- tion and support from one of many breastfeeding support groups. Some are listed below:

LaLeche League International
114 North Meacham Road
Schaumburg, IL 60173-4840
PN: 847-519-7730

LaLeche League Canada
18C Industrial Drive
P.O. Box 29
Chesterville, Ontario KOC1H0
PN: 613-448-1842

LaLeche League Francais
Secretariat General DeLaLLL
C.P. 874
Ville St. Laurent Quebec, H4L4W3
PN: 514-747-9127

International Lactation Consultant Association
200 N. Michigan Ave. Suite 300
Chicago, IL 60601-3821
PN: 312-541-1710

Baby-Friendly USA
8 Jan Sebastian Way #13
Sandwich, MA 02563
PN: 508-888-8044
Web Address: HTTP:WWW.ABOUTUS.COM/A100/BFUSA

Human Milk Banking Association of North America
8 Jan Sebastian Way #13
Sandwich, MA 02563
PN: 508-888-4041 or 1-888-232-8809

We would like to pay a special tribute to the people of the LaLeche League, founded in 1957. This organization has provided consistent, positive support and education to millions of breastfeeding women. If you contact them, you will receive very helpful, experienced advice on the subject of breastfeeding.

In a Perfect World....

You have grown up watching your mother, aunts, and neighbor ladies breastfeeding their infants. It is not uncommon to see women publicly breastfeed their babies, and it is considered a completely natural activity.

When you become pregnant, the decision to breastfeed is not a difficult one; it is a matter of course. Those around you are entirely supportive. Your medical team will give you information about the benefits and management of breastfeeding. The information you take home includes a copy of the hospital's policy on breastfeeding. An appointment with a lactation consultant or breastfeeding specialist is automatically made for you. At this time, she examines your breasts, answers your questions, and provides even more information and resources for you to investigate. During your clinic appointments, any gift packs you receive are completely non-commercial (no free formula).

Your hospital employs an entire staff from nurses to housekeeping personnel who are trained to support lactating mothers. Immediately after delivery, your newborn is placed on your abdomen, and within 30-60 minutes breastfeeding has begun. A nurse or midwife guides you in this important first feeding.

During the postpartum period, your baby is rooming-in with you to give you a chance to fully enjoy mothering. No pacifiers or soothers are used until breastfeeding is well established. All feeding by you is "on demand" so you learn your baby's hunger signals. There is no need for substitute feedings or glucose water. You have started a feeding journal, which you will take to your first postpartum and pediatric appointments. Your pediatrician has examined your baby, met with you, and provided an appointment for a return visit within the first week.

Before being discharged from the hospital, the lactation consultant has again met with you and observed a feeding. She shows you how to pump or express milk, so breastfeeding can be maintained if you need to be away from your baby. You are given information about breastfeeding support groups.

Returning to work, your employer and co-workers are extremely supportive. Adequate time and comfortable facilities for expressing and storing milk are provided.

The feeling of contentment and sheer happiness that accompanies breastfeeding is beyond what you had imagined.

Chapter 8

Complications of Pregnancy

I f you are in generally good health, you can expect a normal pregnancy without major problems. However, a small percent of even the healthiest women develop complications, which are beyond their control to avoid. How these complications are handled by you and your doctor can have a major impact on both you and your baby.

Empowerment doesn't stop when obstacles appear. **You can still retain control of your pregnancy care, even if you develop complications.**

It is not the purpose of this chapter to cover all the possible complications of pregnancy. However, we do want you to know about three in particular, because they are relatively common, and you can have considerable control over your pregnancy care when you have these problems. They are: gestational diabetes, premature labor, and twin pregnancy.

Gestational Diabetes

<u>Diabetes mellitus</u> is a condition where a woman has too much sugar in her blood. Outside of pregnancy, diabetes is a very serious problem, which kills and handicaps many thousands

of people every year. When a woman who has diabetes becomes pregnant, she requires very intensive medical care. But that is not gestational diabetes. <u>Gestational Diabetes Mellitus</u> (GDM) is a diagnosis given to previously healthy women who, during their pregnancies, have higher than normal sugar concentrations in their blood. After the pregnancy, when the hormones of the placenta no longer have any influence on the situation, the blood sugar levels return to their normal, pre-pregnancy levels.

Women with GDM and their babies generally do very well, without major problems. However, their babies are at an increased risk for birth trauma (due to being very large), low blood sugar (hypoglycemia) in the first few days of life, and jaundice in the first week.

Hypoglycemia is a potentially very serious problem, requiring timely care in the nursery. Fortunately, it is easily identifiable and treatable. Jaundice seldom results in long-term problems for the baby. If born prematurely, some babies of mothers with GDM have a difficult time breathing and may need intensive respiratory care for several days.

By far, the main concern your doctor will have when you are diagnosed with gestational diabetes is the possibility that your baby may grow too big. His biggest worry is that your baby will end up with permanent nerve damage after a traumatic and difficult vaginal delivery. He is also worried about being sued if this happens.

Because of these concerns, he is likely to be overly cautious and controlling, resulting in an extraordinary number of blood sugar tests, unnecessary insulin shots, and a higher like-lihood of a cesarean section or induction of labor. Along with this, he may unintentionally impart to you a great deal of anxiety, which is totally undesired and, in many ways, harmful.

Your best "defense", given this situation, is to be well-armed with knowledge. As bad as it may be to blindly accept a doctor's overzealous treatment plan, it is far worse for you and for your baby to foolishly ignore the potential for problems and totally avoid any evaluation or treatment plan. There is a middle ground, and you should be there.

Macrosomia

The term <u>fetal macrosomia</u> basically means that a baby is very big. However, it is difficult, if not impossible, to state categorically how big is "too big." It is a relative term. Pelvic bone architecture varies greatly from woman to woman, and the capacity to deliver large babies, therefore, varies as well.

All obstetricians have seen a rare situation at delivery called "turtling," in which the baby's head comes out but rapidly draws back toward the mother's pelvis, resulting in a very difficult delivery, called Shoulder Dystocia. Under these circumstances, there is usually an atmosphere of panic, as attempt after attempt to deliver the baby's shoulders is met with failure. The baby's head and face turn bluer and bluer, and only minutes may separate them from a dead or neurologically handicapped baby. This is a situation that all obstetricians hate and fear.

When delivered vaginally, some of these babies suffer from fractured clavicles or upper arm bones. Fortunately, these bones heal well within a few weeks, without permanent damage. A small number of these babies will suffer from nerve damage to a shoulder and arm, called Erb's Palsy. Luckily, most babies with Erb's Palsy recover completely, and only a fraction of them will go on to have permanent neurological damage.

Typically, but not always, the kind of baby involved in such a delivery is big and fat, with shoulders and abdomen that are disproportionately large. Such a baby is frequently the child of a woman with diabetes or gestational diabetes. It is therefore understandable that obstetricians worry about fetal macrosomia and GDM.

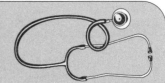

From the Doctor's Files

Infants exposed to many weeks of high sugar levels while in the uterus can get outrageously big. The biggest baby that I have ever seen weighed over 15 pounds at the time of his birth by cesarean. The largest baby I have delivered vaginally weighed 12 pounds, 4 ounces and did well. That mother was not diabetic.

Large baby size is also related to maternal obesity, and it is very difficult to separate that factor from GDM, as the two often go together. Statistically, about 3 out of 1000 deliveries are complicated by shoulder dystocia. In the final analysis, as scary as shoulder dystocia deliveries are, only about 1 baby in 5,000 to 10,000 will end up with permanent neurologic damage as a result of a traumatic delivery due to macrosomia.

Testing for Gestational Diabetes

Somewhere between 1 and 3 percent of pregnant women will have GDM. A small number of those will be discovered to have diabetes mellitus which preceded the pregnancy. Obesity, increased maternal age, a history of big babies, a family history of diabetes, increased amounts of sugar in the urine, and certain ethnic backgrounds all put women at higher risk for having GDM. Women who are from black, Hispanic, or American Indian origins have a considerably higher risk of having GDM than do Caucasian women.

At the present time, more than 90 percent of obstetricians routinely test all their pregnant patients for gestational diabetes.

152

The testing system is not very accurate scientifically, and the results are often not even reproducible on the same woman on different days.

Testing procedures vary somewhat throughout the country. In general, pregnant women are tested at 24 to 28 weeks. They are given a measured amount of a sugar-containing drink, and one hour later, a blood test is taken to measure the blood sugar. It is not necessary, or even advisable, to fast before the blood test.

The woman with a high test result is asked to return on another day for a much more involved blood sugar test, known as a three-hour Glucose Tolerance Test (GTT). This test requires at least four more blood tests. If two or more of these results return as being too high, a diagnosis of GDM is made.

The American College of Obstetricians and Gynecologists (ACOG) does not recommend routine testing of women younger than 25 years old without risk factors, and many doctors do not routinely test their younger pregnant women for gestational diabetes.

Gestational Diabetes Facts:

- Gestational diabetes is not associated with stillborn babies or an increase in neonatal mortality.
- Women under the age of 25 have a very small chance of having GDM, unless they have high risk factors.
- Only 1 baby out of 5000 or so will develop permanent nerve damage from a difficult delivery.
- Testing everyone is very expensive. 15 percent of the women initially tested will require the three-hour GTT. Only 15 percent of those will have an abnormal test result.
- If you passed this test during your last pregnancy, the chance that you have GDM this pregnancy is very small.
- You have every right to decide whether or not to be tested for gestational diabetes.

Dietary Changes

Once GDM has been diagnosed, almost all doctors will, correctly, recommend that their pregnant patients change their diets, in order to decrease the amount of sugar in their blood. The effect of an appropriate diet on lowering a person's blood sugar is usually dramatic. This is when the pregnant woman needs to act responsibly by eating properly and avoiding those foods which will increase her sugar level, and thus the amount of sugar getting to her baby.

Some doctors will only tell their patients to "cut down on the sugar." This kind of dietary advice is simply inadequate. A pregnant women with GDM needs to visit a dietician or nutritionist, and together, they can evaluate her diet, lifestyle, work schedule, habits, etc. The dietician can then put together an appropriate diabetic diet for the pregnant woman to follow. If a dietician is not available, your doctor or his nurse should be able to provide you with some educational material to start you off properly. The basics of a diabetic diet are found in Appendix II.

Most pregnant women with GDM will require nothing more than dietary changes to bring their blood sugar down. However, there are some women who, in spite of being very conscientious about their diets, require insulin shots to keep their blood sugar at acceptable levels. It is important for these women to realize that the need for insulin does not mean that they are guilty of any wrongdoing. The effects of the hormones of pregnancy cause the body to need more insulin as the pregnancy progresses, and some people simply cannot make enough insulin to keep up with their blood sugar needs.

There has recently been some very exciting and encouraging medical news about the safety and effectiveness of taking pills (Glyburide), rather than shots of insulin, to reduce blood sugar levels in pregnancy. This was once thought to be potentially dangerous for the baby, but has now been shown to be safe and effective in pregnancy.

Avoiding Insulin and Frequent Testing

If you develop GDM, there are a few things you can do before you allow yourself to be started on insulin shots or Glyburide, and thus enter into a complex care system of several blood sugar tests every day, frequent fetal testing, and a great deal of aggravating rigmarole.

First and foremost, be honest with yourself. Have you been keeping <u>strictly</u> to a planned diabetic diet, or have you been occasionally eating other foods and snacks? The most common reason why women with GDM end up with high blood sugar is their own dietary indiscretion. If you think you can improve your eating habits, tell your doctor you would like another week to improve your diet so that you might get your blood sugar lower. You might be able to avoid frequent testing and treatment if you do so, and it will make your life a lot simpler and your pregnancy much more enjoyable. Your doctor will appreciate your honesty.

If your blood sugar is then low enough, try to convince your doctor that you will continue to follow the diet strictly, if he will likewise promise to keep you off insulin shots and daily testing. Most doctors will go along with such a plan when it's presented in a cooperative manner.

Secondly, aside from reducing sugar intake, there are other things you can do to lower your blood sugar. The best is to increase your activity. Exercising for 20 to 30 minutes every day will do wonders for bringing high blood sugar down.

Exercise need not be extremely vigorous. Walking 20 to 30 minutes a day is quite sufficient. Even something as simple as 20 minutes a day of arm swings with a two-pound weight in each hand has been shown to minimize the need for insulin. Whatever exercise you choose, keep it moderate and consistent every day.

Another way to reduce blood sugar is to increase the fiber in your diet. At the same time, you will avoid constipation.

Fiber is found in a wide variety of fruits, vegetables, and cereals. Or, if you just want concentrated fiber, many over-the-counter, fiber-containing medications are available, such as Metamucil and Citrucel. Make sure that what you buy is sugar-free.

If the first two plans don't work, find out from your doctor specifically what his goals are for your blood sugar levels. Some doctors can become dictatorial and obsessive about making sure their patient's blood sugar tests are all below 100. This is an unnecessarily rigid goal. A much more rational goal is to keep the majority of your fasting blood sugar tests under 95, and the majority of your two-hour postprandial blood-sugar tests below 120. Most women need to be tested no more than one day a week. It is seldom necessary for a woman who is not taking medicine to be tested several times a day throughout her pregnancy.

Fetal Evaluation Testing

Women with gestational diabetes who don't require insulin treatment don't need prenatal testing of the baby prior to their due dates. And yet, many thousands of these tests are done under those circumstances annually, resulting in a waste of millions of dollars, not to mention the stress these women live with from week to week, worrying about their babies. Interestingly, increasing stress will also increase a person's blood sugar, making the situation even more complicated than it needs to be.

Some of these women will undergo an amniocentesis to evaluate fetal lung maturity. This is not only unnecessary, assuming there are no additional indications, but has a slight potential to be harmful, due to possible injury from the needle.

Ultrasound estimation of fetal weight is frequently used to decide the route of delivery. A cesarean delivery should be strongly considered if the baby weighs more than 9 1/2 pounds. This decision, of course, depends on other factors as well, especially maternal pelvic bone structure. If the baby is felt to be obviously small enough to pass through the space available, then ultrasound may not be necessary.

Induction of Labor

The vast majority of women with GDM should be allowed to go into labor spontaneously and deliver normally. In years past, there was a general recommendation, based on very little hard evidence, that these women should not go past their due dates. This led to a lot of women being unsuccessfully induced and ending up with unnecessary cesarean sections or long, painful labors.

That recommendation has changed somewhat, so that now, instead of inducing labor on all these women near their due dates, fetal assessment tests are done twice a week after the due date until they either go into labor or their cervix becomes ready for induction. This has allowed for more normal labors and deliveries for these women.

If you have gestational diabetes controlled by diet alone, try to avoid an induction of labor if your cervix is closed or very long or firm. If your only problem is GDM, induction under these circumstances is not usually necessary and may lead to a long labor or an unwanted cesarean section. However, as GDM is sometimes complicated by additional problems, such as increased blood pressure, preeclampsia, fetal macrosomia, etc., it is important to discuss this in detail with your doctor.

Health Risks for the Woman

Women who develop GDM have an increased risk of developing diabetes outside of pregnancy in the years to come. It is important for women who required insulin or Glyburide during their pregnancy to have their blood sugar tested outside of pregnancy. A good time to do this is at the six-week postpartum visit. At that time, a fasting blood sugar can be done. If the level is 126 or higher, further consultation with a diabetic specialist is needed.

Even if the test at six weeks is normal, the increased risk for the future is still there. Continuing the diabetic diet, losing weight when appropriate, and continuing a mild exercise program will reduce those risks considerably. **Avoiding diabetes outside of pregnancy is a very worthwhile goal and may be one of the best reasons to get a blood sugar test done during your pregnancy.** If you developed GDM, you should get blood sugar tests done with your future annual exams.

Next Pregnancy

Women who have GDM in one pregnancy are likely to have it again in the next pregnancy and all that follow. This is not always true, however. Many women with GDM have had perfectly normal blood sugar levels in their following pregnancies by losing weight and sticking to the basics of a diabetic diet.

For those women whose blood sugar outside of pregnancy is too high, special advice about folic acid is needed. High maternal blood sugar in early pregnancy is associated with an increased risk of having a baby with congenital defects. Taking folic acid (a vitamin) prior to and during early pregnancy will reduce those risks considerably. (See Chapter 3.)

Premature Labor

Preterm delivery is by far the most significant major medical problem in pregnancy.

Premature or preterm (the words are often used interchangeably) babies represent only 9 percent of the babies born, but make up 90 percent of the babies in intensive-care nurseries, 75 percent of the normal babies who die, and more than 50 percent of babies who develop cerebral palsy, mental retardation, or other major permanent neurologic handicaps.

Care of preterm infants is also very expensive. The average hospital costs for a baby born 14 weeks early is in the range of $150,000-250,000. The lifetime financial costs involved in the medical care of a preterm child who develops cerebral palsy are well into the millions. All in all, preterm babies account for many billions of dollars in medical care costs every year in the United States.

From the Nurse's Notes

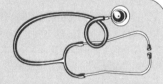

The emotional impact of having a significantly preterm baby is usually overwhelming. Seeing your tiny, skinny, helpless baby being constantly subjected to needles, tubes, wires, noises, and strange lights just to keep him alive is a terrifying experience, especially at first.

Preterm delivery is number one on every obstetrician's list of things to avoid, if possible. Because obstetricians understand the seriousness of the problem, they are zealous about trying to stop or delay preterm labor. Unfortunately, quite often, they are too zealous and our pregnant patients are the ones who suffer unnecessarily.

Real Preterm Labor

Preterm labor is defined as regular uterine contractions, five to eight minutes, or less, apart, occurring between 20 and 36 weeks, accompanied by one or more of the following:

- Progressive cervical changes (opening and/or thinning).
- Cervical dilatation of 2 cm or more.
- Cervical effacement (thinning) of 80% percent or more.

It is very important to note that frequent contractions without changes in the cervix do not constitute preterm labor.

There are many reasons why pregnant women may have frequent uterine contractions and not really be in labor. Intercourse or other sexual stimulation, minor abdominal trauma, viral infections anywhere in the body, urinary-tract infections, food poisoning, dehydration, and excessive physical activity can all lead to frequent, but clinically unimportant, contractions. This is false preterm labor.

If you have very frequent contractions, i.e., more than twenty in two consecutive hours prior to 36 weeks (one month early), it is very important to be seen and evaluated by your doctor. Without an examination of your cervix, you will not know if this is the real deal or just false preterm labor. Do not gamble and assume anything. See your doctor.

Real preterm labor has many possible causes. A common cause is uterine or cervical infection. The more we learn about preterm labor, the more we realize how frequently infection plays a part in causing it. Premature rupture of the membranes (broken bag of water) is a major cause of preterm labor and is frequently caused by infection.

Partial placental separation, twin pregnancy, abnormal configuration of the uterus or cervix, too much amniotic fluid, a variety of medical illnesses, cocaine use, cigarette smoking, and fetal and placental abnormalities round out the top of the list of reasons for real preterm labor.

<u>Real</u> preterm labor usually leads to <u>real</u> preterm delivery. <u>False</u> preterm labor does not. Real preterm labor sometimes needs real treatment, but not always. Quite often, it is far better for the baby to be in the environment of a neonatal intensive-care unit (NICU) than in the infected or sickly environment of a prematurely laboring uterus. Real preterm labor is often Nature's way of telling us that this baby needs to come out for its own good.

Obstetricians, if they are doing their jobs properly, will try to evaluate which babies need to be delivered promptly and which to try to delay. As any pediatrician will tell you, he would rather take care of an otherwise healthy 30-week baby than a sickly, infected 33-week baby.

False Preterm Labor

Initially, it is often difficult to be certain if a woman is in real or false preterm labor. In those cases, it is usually wise, if in doubt, to err on the side of caution. Evaluation will usually clear up the confusion, and treatment can then be continued or stopped. Unfortunately, since false preterm labor is so much more common than real preterm labor, many pregnant women are inappropriately receiving medication and treatment for long periods of time. They are subjected to aggravating and potentially dangerous medications, countless weeks of bed rest, hours upon hours of fruitless home uterine monitoring, unnecessary anxiety, and frequent loss of income and companionship all due to overzealous treatment of contractions without cervical change, i.e. <u>false</u> preterm labor. We don't want this to happen to you.

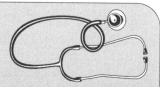

From the Doctor's Files

I can't even count the number of patients I've seen, in consultation or after the fact, who have been taking tocolytics (medications to stop contractions) and at bed rest for weeks on end, only to go on to a full-term delivery, weeks after discontinuing the treatment. Overtreatment of preterm contractions is the rule rather than the exception in American obstetrics.

Indications for Treatment

To be sure, there are some women and babies who benefit from long-term use of tocolysis and/or bed rest. Women who may benefit from this treatment almost always have one of the following problems:

- Thin or dilated cervix.
- Fetal head low in pelvis.
- Bleeding due to a poorly attached placenta.
- Twin pregnancy with a gradually dilating cervix.

Other problems which benefit from intensive, prolonged tocolysis and bed rest, are rare. Long-term bed rest results in a variety of parallel problems—child care troubles, muscle wasting, loss of money from a job (or loss of the job itself), psychological and physical dependency, depression, increased risk of phlebitis, loss of companionship, and so on. **Long-term bed rest is very difficult, usually detrimental, and often totally unnecessary**. However, your bed rest does make your doctor feel better.

If you get directions from your physician for total bed rest for any extended period of time, i.e., more than a few days, you should question him directly about the real need for it. Unless your cervix is dilated or thinned out, or you have major bleeding problems, there are very few reasons why you should need prolonged bed rest.

Probably 75 percent of women treated for more than one week with tocolytics are being overtreated, and probably 90 percent or more of women at total bed rest for more than a few days are doing themselves more harm than good.

There are many different causes for real preterm labor, and every pregnant woman's circumstances are unique and require individualized evaluation. There is no way any book or magazine article can tell you what you should do in every circumstance. This is what we have doctors for. You want your doctor to give you the best possible care, and so do we.

Sexual Intercourse and Contractions

In addition to bed rest and tocolytic medications for your preterm labor problems, your doctor may tell you to avoid intercourse. Intercourse, semen, and orgasm all increase contractions. If you are at high risk for preterm delivery because your cervix is open and/or thinning, intercourse may start up real preterm labor.

If you have been troubled by false preterm labor and your cervix is closed and long, intercourse will rarely, if ever, lead to a preterm delivery. You may, however, notice contractions after intercourse.

Testing for Premature Labor Risk

In the next few years, the use of vaginal ultrasound to evaluate the cervix and a new test called fibronectin will result in a major change in how obstetricians evaluate and treat preterm labor. Real preterm labor requires changes in the cervix. By using vaginal ultrasound it is possible to measure these changes down to the nearest millimeter. This technology is available now and is very helpful in discriminating between false and real preterm labor. You may get a vaginal ultrasound scan of your cervix for clarification if there is any doubt about your preterm labor problem. If your cervix is at least 3 cm long and closed, you are most likely dealing with false preterm labor.

A test for a substance called fibronectin is now publicly available. When fibronectin is present in vaginal or cervical secretions, the risk of real premature labor within the next several weeks is relatively high. On the other hand, if you are having frequent contractions, but fibronectin is absent from the vaginal secretions, preterm delivery is very unlikely. The exact role of the test in pregnancy management has yet to be clarified, but it will be an important part of obstetric care in the early 21st century.

Twins

Being pregnant with twins is simultaneously exciting and scary, enjoyable and aggravating, wonderful and dreadful. In comparison, however, the first year of raising twins makes the pregnancy seem easy. All together, this will probably be the most physically and emotionally demanding time that a woman will ever experience.

The quality of your obstetric care during a twin pregnancy may have a great impact on your life and the lives of your children. Twin pregnancies are, by their very nature, frequently very complicated, requiring all the knowledge and experience of your obstetrician and his health-care team. If you are pregnant with twins, your best chance for a good outcome is to seek prenatal care from an obstetrician or perinatologist (high-risk obstetrician), especially one who can also provide you the services of a dietician, an obstetric nurse educator, and a social worker. Trusting the lives of your twins to most family physicians or midwives is risky, as most of them do not have the expertise or resources you will need.

From the Nurse's Notes

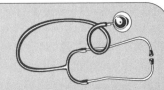

Most couples expecting twins have no family history of multiple births. The idea that having twins skip a generation simply isn't true. A family history of twins only minimally increases the chances, but certainly there are isolated families with more than their fair share of multiple births.

Under natural circumstances, about one-third of twins are identical and the other two-thirds are fraternal, or non-identical. However, now that highly sophisticated infertility treatments are resulting in more multiple births, the percentage of identical twins is slowly decreasing. The vast majority of twins con-

ceived with ovulation enhancing medications comes from separately fertilized eggs, leading to fraternal twins.

Diet

If you are pregnant with twins you will need special dietary treatment. To begin with, an additional 300 calories per day will be required. A weight gain of 35 to 45 pounds is the average for a twin pregnancy, compared to about 25 to 30 pounds for a singleton. A discussion with a nutritionist can help you determine how to best achieve that goal.

Premature Labor

Special treatment also means intense education on the signs and symptoms of premature labor, which is by far the most significant medical problem in a twin pregnancy. Twins only represent about 2 percent of all babies, but make up about 10 percent of the babies in the neonatal intensive care units across the country. The average twin pregnancy lasts about 36 to 37 weeks compared to 40 weeks for one baby. It is rare for twins to get to their full-term due date.

Women who are pregnant with twins fall into two basic categories: Those who have no problems with preterm labor and those with frequent preterm labor problems, which invariably lead to early delivery. The difference between these two groups is usually determined by the length of the woman's cervix. If a woman has a long (more than 3 cm), closed cervix at 24 weeks, she has little chance of problems with significant preterm labor and delivery. She may continue to be active and lead a reasonably normal life, in spite of having twins.

On the other hand, women whose cervices are shorter than 3 cm at about 24 weeks or shows signs of "funneling" of the cervix can expect a great deal of trouble with preterm labor. "Funneling" refers to the gradual opening of the upper, inner portion of the cervix, which can only be identified with ultrasound. This ultrasound scan can be extremely helpful in determining what risk category you fall into. If your obstetrician schedules this procedure for you, you know he is on top of the situation. If not, you can suggest it. It may make a tremendous difference in the health of your babies.

Benefits of Treatment

For those women with short cervices, a variety of treatments can prolong the pregnancy and result in healthier babies. These treatments are aimed at decreasing contractions and relieving pressure on the cervix. This is one of the few situations where moderate bed rest may actually be helpful.

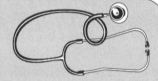

From the Doctor's Files

I have been very impressed by the beneficial effects of a medicine called indomethacin for preterm labor. Not only does it relax the uterus, it also keeps pressure off the cervix by reducing the amount of amniotic fluid.

By utilizing indomethacin before 32 weeks, doing frequent cervical and amniotic fluid evaluations by ultrasound, and through intensive nursing education and support, we have managed to keep our antenatal hospitalization and premature delivery rates quite low, and thus, our neonatal outcomes are excellent. In comparison to other perinatal centers reporting twin pregnancy outcomes, we do very well utilizing this outpatient approach.

I like to think that our excellent statistics for twin pregnancy outcomes are due, in part, to the system of care that our women get, including supportive and educational services and the use of vaginal ultrasound for cervical evaluation with the use of the indomethacin when indicated.

Labor & Delivery

When two babies occupy one uterus, they often get into odd positions, which may lead to difficult situations at the time of delivery. For this reason, cesarean section rates for twins are considerably higher than for singletons. Nationally, these rates vary dramatically, from about 30 to 75 percent. You should ask your doctor about his cesarean rate for twins. If it is higher than 50 percent, you should find out why. Many cesareans for twins are done unnecessarily.

When the Second Baby is Breech

One of the ongoing controversies in obstetric care is the appropriate type of delivery for twins when the first baby is head down and the second is not. This happens in about 25 percent of twin pregnancies. Many obstetricians will always suggest doing the cesarean section under this circumstance, but this is not usually necessary.

If you find yourself in this situation, you should know that the outcome for babies in this setting is the same, whether they are delivered vaginally or by cesarean section. Much depends on the experience of the obstetrician in delivering second twins and the anesthesia available.

Most of the time, second babies who are breech will drift down after the first baby has been delivered, so that their buttocks are in the pelvis. Delivery of these breech babies is usually quick because the first baby has just stretched out the mother's cervix, muscles, and other tissues.

With good anesthesia (either epidural, spinal, or brief general anesthesia), a second baby can usually be delivered safely, regardless of position. The doctor can reach up inside the uterus and grab the baby's feet and pull, if necessary. The rest of the baby follows easily. Many obstetricians are afraid to deliver any breech babies, for reasons of fear of malpractice suits and/or inexperience. The more often pregnant women request vaginal breech deliveries, the fewer unnecessary cesarean sections will be performed.

Pediatricians in the Delivery Room

It is important that adequate pediatric personnel are present in the delivery room to handle any resuscitation needed for a second twin. This kind of necessary support system is frequently not found in small hospitals, and that is one of the main reasons why twins should be delivered in larger hospitals.

From the Doctor's Files

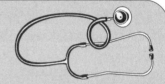

Having the opportunity to care for many women with twins has given me the chance to be part of some amazing and poignant stories, such as Sue Barnett's:

Heroes in the movies come and go frequently, but real heroes are rare, and our memories of them stay with us forever.

I experienced a rare opportunity to meet a real hero, one who gave up his own life so his two brothers could live. His name was William Andrew Barnett, and he fit in the palm of my hand.

When I first met Sue and Bob Barnett in September of 1995, she was 11 weeks pregnant and couldn't keep from smiling. She had reason to be happy, for she and her husband had been trying to have a baby for nearly ten years, and finally it seemed as though their long wait would soon be over.

Her only previous pregnancy, in 1991, had ended sadly with a miscarriage. Four years and three operations later, after an in vitro fertilization procedure, Sue and Bob were expecting. And they were expecting a lot, triplets to be exact. As we listened to the three little heartbeats that day, none of us could know what difficulties lay ahead. We just smiled at each other and enjoyed the moment.

Sue had experienced problems with fibroids in her uterus. These are usually insignificant, small, round growths of varying size on the uterine muscle, which are frequently noted in women over 34. However, in some women, including Sue, they can cause a variety of reproductive problems.

A few years before, she'd had some fibroids removed from her uterus, during an operation designed to help her achieve a pregnancy. The surgery had not been successful. More fibroids had formed and no pregnancy had ensued. And now, finally, she was pregnant, but the fibroids were there, lurking, waiting to cause trouble.

Normally, pregnant women with uterine fibroids experience no particular problems, but Sue was not so lucky. At about 17 weeks into her pregnancy, she began having a lot of pain on the left side of her rapidly enlarging uterus. The fibroid located there, which two months earlier had been quite small, had now tripled in size and was not only causing pain, but also contractions.

She was given large doses of indomethacin to decrease the local inflammation and keep the uterus relaxed, but it wasn't working very well. She continued to contract, and her cervix began to thin and open. Sue was in labor at eighteen weeks (four and a half months), and there didn't seem to be much we could do about it.

This process dragged on for a couple of days, and, as her cervix gradually dilated, hope for these babies' survival was rapidly vanishing. The earliest possibility for survival for any premature baby is at 23 weeks, and that was still five weeks away.

On the morning of November 11, Sue told me that she was feeling an increase in pelvic pressure. When I examined her, I found a baby in her vagina, just waiting to come out. With one push, little William Andrew Barnett, weighing only 7.6 ounces, was born. As I held him in the palm of my hand, I marveled at the vigorous movements of his tiny arms and legs in his desperate struggle to survive. But he was far too young to live very long, and he died in his father's arms only a few hours later.

After William Andrew's birth, Sue's uterus stopped contracting, and her cervix thickened and closed so that it was only open about 2 cm. This was a welcome surprise to both of us and allowed us an opportunity to have a glimmer of hope for the survival of her two remaining babies.

Over the next 24 hours, we waited anxiously to see what would happen. I gave her some antibiotics, continued the indomethacin, and watched while her uterus remained relaxed and her pain began to subside. That fibroid of hers had grown so quickly that the middle of it was dying, a process well known to obstetricians as degeneration. During degeneration, a large amount of hormone called prostaglandin is produced. This hormone causes labor. Once the degeneration process wanes, contractions disappear. This is what was happening to Sue. Her uterus, under these circumstances, could apparently tolerate only two babies. Three was one too many.

We were unable to save William Andrew, but there was hope 24 hours later that, by putting stitches around her cervix, we might prolong the pregnancy by several weeks. But five weeks was such a long time! I had read about occasional successes in cases such as this, but rarely did those pregnancies last more than a few weeks. Perhaps it was too much to hope for.

Sue, Bob, and I had a long talk about the cervical stitches (called a cerclage), and the unlikely, but still possible, chance that we could keep her pregnancy going for such a long time. They had been through a lot emotionally and physically, but weren't about to give up. They gave me the go ahead to put in the cerclage.

The procedure was technically simple. The placenta and cord William Andrew left behind were still in place. I put some suture around that cord as high as I could, cut off the lower part of it, and put the remaining cord back up inside the uterus. Two stitches around the cervix closed it up like a purse-string.

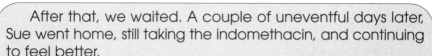

After that, we waited. A couple of uneventful days later, Sue went home, still taking the indomethacin, and continuing to feel better.

Days turned to weeks. During that time, Sue did a few things around the house, but kept relatively inactive. The 23-week milestone came and went. We started smiling again. Amazingly, 11 weeks after the stitches were put in, Sue was still pregnant. At 29 weeks, the outlook for her babies was very optimistic, and I was almost giddy with our apparent success. I should have known that trouble was again on the way.

In late January, 28 weeks into the pregnancy, Sue again began having frequent contractions and her cervix slowly, but progressively, started to dilate and thin out.

On January 29, 1996, she came to see me with more intense cramping than she'd had before. When I examined her cervix, I found it to be 3 cm dilated and completely thinned out. I felt something odd between the baby's head and the cervix. As I pondered what it was, I noticed that it was pulsating and felt like a large worm all coiled up at the end of my fingers. I then realized that this was the umbilical cord of that baby trying to come out first.

Ordinarily, when a woman has preterm labor at 29 weeks, we try to stop the contractions with medicine. However, in Sue's case, if her membranes ruptured, that cord could get fully compressed within minutes, cutting off all oxygen to the baby, resulting in its death. We had gotten too far, and she had gone through too much to risk that.

Within minutes, we were preparing for a cesarean section under epidural anesthesia. At 9:56 a.m., Kellin Andrew was born, weighing 2 pounds, 15 1/2 ounces and crying vigorously. Very soon thereafter, Robert William, also screaming, was born. He weighed 3 pounds, 1 ounce. Sue and her babies did very well after delivery. When I last saw them, the boys were two years old and healthy. They owe their lives to a very small hero they once knew, but will never see. Together, they will carry his name, so that he will always be with them.

Chapter 9

Domestic Abuse

Every year, somewhere between two and four million American women are assaulted by their partners. Nearly five thousand are killed, and untold thousands fear for their lives every day. Pregnancy provides no protection from the abusers. It is estimated that 6-15 percent of all pregnant women suffer from emotional, sexual, or physical violence.

If this concerns you, the most important thing to know is that pregnancy can be a time when you will have an opportunity to become empowered to provide a safe environment for yourself and your baby. **There are many sources of help for you if you live with domestic abuse**.

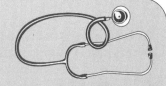

From the Doctor's Files

All obstetricians and midwives see many women who suffer from domestic violence. I would like to share Becky Shepard's story with you, in order to illustrate the seriousness of the problem.

The last time I saw Becky Shepard, she was still alive. Being her obstetrician, our last visit together was her six-week postpartum appointment, and we talked about the usual stuff—the baby, birth control, sleepless nights, and so on. It really wasn't possible to talk about her main problem, because he was in the room with us at all times.

Our relationship had gone back to the beginning of her second pregnancy, when they came to see me for an initial obstetric visit. Her first baby was stillborn, and no one could figure out why. During that visit, it was hard not to notice her boyfriend, Nick, because he did most of the talking, answering most of the questions I directed toward Becky. It was easy to see that theirs was a relationship of control, and Becky was on the wrong side of it. Even when I did the physical exam, including the pelvic exam, he was there, sitting and watching with his arms crossed and a scowl on his face.

At every following prenatal visit, Nick was there, dominating the conversation, answering her questions, and making all the decisions. This guy was not only annoying, he was a little scary. I felt sorry for Becky. I wanted to see Becky alone, so I could talk with her about any problems regarding domestic abuse or violence, but I couldn't bring up the subject with him right there.

In spite of the lack of evidence of physical violence, I was concerned about her. I shared my concern with one of our nurses, Sheri, who suggested that I send Becky to the rest room to empty her bladder prior to a pelvic exam late in the pregnancy. She would do the rest. Nick was pretty controlling, but even he didn't follow her into the women's rest room. Sheri did though. It was in the women's rest room that Becky was interviewed, very quickly, and very privately, regarding our concerns about domestic abuse. Sheri was able to confirm that my suspicions were correct.

One day, near the due date, Sheri and Becky stayed in the rest room for a long, long time. I knew Nick would know that something fishy was going on, so I went over to the women's room and put my ear to the door (I wonder what that looked like) and heard a lot of crying. I knew this would not be over soon, so I went to Nick and told him that I had sent Becky to the lab for a test. He cussed under his breath and went to the lab, one floor down, to look for her.

Somehow everything glossed over pretty well, in spite of all the awkwardness. After they left, I went to Sheri, who was herself red-eyed from crying.

"That bastard killed her first baby," she sputtered angrily. "He beat her up and kicked her in the abdomen at the end of the pregnancy, and after that, the baby stopped moving."

We did what we could to help Becky. We got her to talk; we listened; we provided resources. Becky was in a dangerous situation, and was coping the best she could. Sheri had given her lots of information about the local shelter for battered women and her legal recourses, but Becky had to take the first step on her own.

Shortly after that, Becky went into labor and had a beautiful baby girl. Nick stayed with her in the hospital, and I had no private time with her. I had arranged a visiting nurse to go to the house for the first few weeks after delivery, but she didn't report anything out of the ordinary. When we had our last visit together, six weeks after the baby was born, I didn't know how this would all turn out.

One year later, on the front page of the newspaper, I saw her picture. The story said that she was missing. Nick had told the police that she had just left one day without the baby and didn't return. There was no trace of her. No evidence of any kind has shown up in the years since then, but Sheri, Nick, and I know what happened to her. The police also suspect Nick of killing her, but they don't have evidence for a conviction. Now, he has a new girlfriend.

Pregnancy and Domestic Violence

Because pregnancy is a time when domestic violence against women escalates, we obstetricians have ample opportunities to see battered and abused women of all races and social classes. We would like to be able to tell you that Becky Shepard's story is rare, but sadly, we cannot.

During pregnancy, women are emotionally and physically vulnerable. It is also a time when abused women have an opportunity to obtain information, support, and, when needed, referrals to community resources for help, when help is needed the most. Miscarriages, stillbirths, and other complications of pregnancy are more common for the abused pregnant woman.

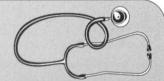

From the Nurse's Notes

Domestic abuse encompasses far more than just physical trauma. It is an insidious process of demoralizing enslavement of the mind and body by the partner, who uses physical, psychological, and frequently, sexual abuse to attain absolute power and control in the relationship. It affects women of all races and social classes.

We occasionally have seen women with bruises, scars, and even old cigarette burns as mementos of recent or past abuses. These visible scars are minor in comparison to the emotional scars they carry.

Emotional abuse as a means of control frequently takes the form of insults, criticism, intimidation, false accusations, and refusal to help during illnesses or injuries. Whether the actions are physical, emotional, or sexual, intimidation and degradation are the cornerstones of domestic abuse.

As a general rule, the abuse, possessiveness, and jealousy increases, and physical and social isolation become even more obvious during pregnancy. The abuser controls what his partner reads, where she goes, how much money she has, and with whom she talks.

Are you becoming a victim of domestic abuse?

- Does your partner threaten you or throw things when he is angry?
- Has he physically hurt you in the past year?
- Does he blame you for his violence?
- Has he forced you to perform a sexual act?
- Do you feel that you deserve the abusive treatment?

Many of you reading this will recognize these characteristics in your present or past relationships. If so, you too are, or have been, affected by domestic abuse. **If we are describing your present relationship with your partner, you need to know that you are not alone and that help is available.** Life can be better, but unless you do something about your situation, it will undoubtedly get worse. **No one deserves to be battered.**

Your Doctor's Role

Over the last several years, major medical organizations, such as the American College of Obstetrics and Gynecology, have been encouraging doctors to ask all of their female patients about domestic abuse. We know that one-third of women suffering from depression, one-fourth of women seen in emergency rooms, and a significant number of women with chronic problems, such as debilitating headaches and pelvic pain, are suffering primarily from domestic abuse.

177

Unfortunately, even when given an opportunity to reveal their problem to us, victimized women are frequently reluctant to do so. This is often due to the fear of the consequences should their partners find out. But there are other reasons as well, such as shame and humiliation, religious or ethnic constraints, extremely poor self-esteem, economic worries and, often, the belief or hope that things will get better on their own.

Another major barrier to open discussion of domestic abuse may be the physician's difficulties in addressing the issue. He is likely to avoid the subject entirely during pregnancy because of a lack of awareness or a feeling of inadequacy in solving the problem.

A common reaction medical professionals and others have when confronted by a woman describing her abusive relationship is to try the quick fix. "Why don't you just leave him?" is the usual verbal prescription, but it isn't as simple as that.

In fact, **the most dangerous time for an abused woman is at the time of separation or threat of separation.** It is then that the abuser tries to exert the most physical control, and this can be deadly. Being pregnant gives an abused woman a chance to seek and receive information, counseling and assistance. All doctor's offices have contacts with social service agencies, advocacy programs, or hospital-based intervention programs, which may be lifesaving.

Your doctor or his nurse can give you written information, (including telephone numbers) about legal options, local counseling, crisis and intervention services, shelters and other community resources.

There are national organizations which are helpful as well. The National Domestic Violence Hotline (1-800-333-SAFE) is a 24-hour resource to help women find local shelters. The Family Violence Prevention Fund (1-415-821-4555) provides direct services to victims, in addition to developing public policy and training programs.

It is very important that your abusive partner is not aware of your efforts to seek assistance. If he is, your personal safety or the safety of your children may be in jeopardy. Any and all discussions with doctors or nurses on this matter must be done in private. Also, remember that children can overhear things and repeat them at awkward times.

Whether your doctor initiates a discussion on domestic violence or not, your prenatal visit to his office may open a window of opportunity for you to seek help if you are abused. That open window may save your life.

Preparation may be critical when there is a possibility of violence. You cannot prevent your partner's violent actions, but you can prepare how best to respond, so you can get yourself and your children to safety.

Violent behavior danger signs:

- Yelling, taunting, name-calling
- Threatening to harm children or pets
- Threatening the use of a weapon
- Escalating the level of abuse with each episode
- Threatening to kill you

Use any or all of these planned safety strategies:
- Practice how to get out of your house or apartment safely.
- Keep your purse and car keys in a place where you can quickly and reliably grab them.
- Tell a neighbor in advance to call the police if they hear suspicious noises coming from your house or apartment.
- Hide a cell phone (often provided by shelters or police departments) where you will be able to get to it.
- Teach your children how and when to call the police.
- Have a place to go that you know will be safe.

- When an argument begins, move automatically to a room with an exit. The most violent domestic abuse occurs in rooms with no exit, such as bathrooms, bedrooms, and garages.
- Avoid rooms with weapons. The kitchen has a lot of weapons. Do not plan on using a weapon for safety. These are almost always taken away and used against the battered woman.

Preparation can be very empowering.

Safety when Preparing to Leave your Partner

This is typically one of the most dangerous times in an abusive relationship. In order to maximize your safety, plan in advance.

- Leave money, important documents, and keys with a close friend or relative who will be available when you leave.
- Open your own checking or savings account in advance. Have the monthly statements sent to another address (friend, relative, etc.).
- Be prepared to call your local domestic violence hot line number for help.
- Make sure you have access to a telephone.
- Have a confidential place to go. Your partner may try to find you in some of the more obvious places. Violence can occur there also.
- Leave some extra clothing for yourself and your children where you can get to it.
- Mentally and physically rehearse your escape plan.

Items to take when leaving

- Driver's license and registration.
- Money.
- Checkbook, ATM card.
- Credit cards.
- Keys to house, car, and office.
- Medications.
- Address book.
- Pictures.
- Children's favorite toys or blankets.
- Items of sentimental value.
- Jewelry.
- Any other important papers such as birth certificates (yours and children's), social security card, passport, and welfare identification.

Safety after your partner leaves

- Change the locks on the doors as soon as possible.
- Teach the children how to phone you or someone else you trust if your partner takes them away.
- Make sure that the children's school, day care, and baby-sitters know who is and who is not permitted to pick them up.
- Inform a neighbor to call the police if your partner is seen near your residence.

Restraining Orders

In many domestic abuse situations, an injunction called a restraining order is obtained through the police and court system. Its purpose is to have a legal safety mechanism to discourage the abusive partner from physical contact with the battered woman. Sometimes the threat of jail works well to keep the abuser away. Sometimes it doesn't.

If you have a restraining order against your partner, here are some simple safety measures:

- Keep your restraining order with you or near you.
- If you work in or frequently visit other communities, notify the police departments there of your restraining order. A restraining order issued in one county is good in any county.
- Keep in touch with the people in your local domestic violence programs and make sure you know your legal rights.
- Inform your employer, building security supervisor, close friends, and relatives of your restraining order and what it means.
- Call the police if your partner violates the restraining order. Even if he is very friendly at first contact, he is a dangerous person. Protect yourself and call the police quickly.
- Avoid going to the stores, banks, bars, and restaurants he will expect you to use.

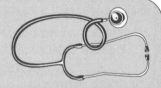

From the Nurse's Notes

Battered women, pregnant or not, frequently feel confused and dependent. Take the time to plan these basic safety steps, which will make you more focused and independent. They may also save your life.

Chapter 10

Breech Babies

At the end of a full-term pregnancy, about 97 percent of babies are in the vertex (head down) position and ready for a normal delivery. The other 3 percent are nearly all in the breech (buttocks or feet first) position. Since there are about four million babies born in the United States every year, this means that roughly 120,000 mothers a year find themselves in this potentially troublesome situation.

For those of you in this situation, you need to know that **having a breech baby does not necessarily need to result in a cesarean section.**

The biggest and therefore most difficult part of the baby to deliver is its head. When the baby comes down head first, and the head comes out, we know the rest of the baby will follow. In breech babies, the head is the last part to come out, so when we deliver the legs and the body, we don't know for sure that the baby's head will also come out so easily. There is usually a moment of considerable anxiety as manipulations are done to accomplish delivery of the baby's arms and head. This is as true for those of us who have considerable experience with breech deliveries, as it is for those doctors who have only delivered a few.

Delivering a breech baby can be a very simple or a very complicated procedure, depending on many variables. The position of the baby's legs, arms, and head, coupled with the size and shape of the mother's pelvis, all make for a variety of very interesting circumstances, not all of which are conducive to a safe vaginal delivery.

The Role of an Experienced Obstetrician

It is important that the doctor who is assisting in the breech delivery has the experience that is necessary to know how to deal with the intricacies and difficulties, which may develop. It is much safer for a breech baby to be delivered by cesarean section than to have an obstetrician, inexperienced in breech deliveries, attempt to deliver it vaginally.

Unfortunately, doctors experienced in delivering breech babies are becoming hard to find. For the past 20 years or so, there has been a trend in the United States toward delivering all breech babies by cesarean section. This has resulted in fewer and fewer obstetricians learning the technique of breech delivery during their training. We now realize that many babies can be born safely in the breech position, but there are few doctors willing and able to deliver them.

Now that we have scared you away from vaginal breech delivery, let me bring you back to the truth, which is that most babies in the breech position at term can be safely delivered vaginally. There are many things, which experienced obstetricians evaluate before even considering vaginal delivery.

Different Baby Positions

The position of the baby's legs is very important. Babies whose feet are up by their ears (frank breech position) are the best candidates for a vaginal delivery for a couple of very good reasons (see figure 9). First, the likelihood of the umbilical cord causing problems (cord prolapse) with a frank breech is very small. Second, as the baby comes down into the mother's pelvis, the combined circumference of the baby's chest and the adjacent legs is approximately equal to that of the head. Therefore, if they make it through, the head follows nicely and "voila!" we have a baby. Since most term breech babies are in this position, most will do well with a vaginal delivery.

Figure 9
Frank Breech

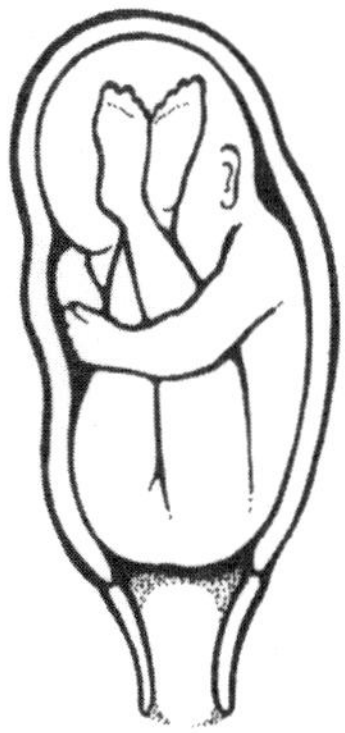

Other positions of the baby's legs are potentially more troublesome. Sometimes, babies seem to be trying to walk out, i.e., they come feet first. This is called a double footling breech position. This is the worst position of all the breeches (see figure 10), because the risk of cord prolapse is quite high (11 percent). This is the kind of problem that can kill babies and therefore it understandably leads to emergency cesarean sections. The other problem with this position is that the head may get trapped after the legs and abdomen are partially delivered. Nobody needs this kind of aggravation. If your baby is trying to come out feet first, forget about vaginal breech delivery and be happy with a cesarean and a healthy baby.

Figure 10
Footling Breech

Another interesting position is called complete breech. This is when the baby appears to be sitting on its feet (see figure 11). This situation is somewhere in between frank breech and double footling breech in terms of risk and safety. Most obstetricians who do vaginal breech deliveries will only do so if the baby is frank breech, but some will also include complete breech babies.

Figure 11
Complete Breech

Size of the Breech Baby

Of course, the size of the baby is a very important part of the decision-making process. Very large breech babies can have very difficult and traumatic deliveries. Surprisingly, very small breech babies also have troubles. This is because they are nearly always quite premature, and their head size is disproportionately large compared to the rest of their bodies. The incompletely dilated cervix can actually trap the baby's head and keep it from coming out. This usually results in a disastrous situation for the baby.

My experience, and that of many doctors who have gone before me, shows that delivering very premature breech babies vaginally can be very dangerous. We rarely do it in the United States if the baby is less than 3 1/2 pounds or so, or about 32 weeks.

In addition to the positions of the legs, the size of the mother's pelvis may be crucial for a safe breech delivery. If you had a 9-pound baby before, and this breech baby is only about 7 or 8 pounds, it should come out easily. However, having had a baby before does not guarantee safety for a breech delivery the next time around.

There are some other factors which help us decide whether or not a breech baby can be delivered safely, such as the amount of extension of the baby's neck, presence of the cord around the neck, certain fetal abnormalities, etc. Without getting too deep into the many details and possible variations, it is safe to say that a doctor will be considering a lot of variables in preparation for a breech delivery.

Turning the Baby Around

All of this can be avoided, however, if we can figure out a way to get the baby into the position we all would like to see: head down. This is a real possibility and should be considered for all breech babies in the last month of pregnancy. The procedure is called external version. During the procedure, the baby is turned from a breech (or transverse) position to a head down (vertex) position. If successful, this will allow for a very good chance for a normal delivery, instead of a high likelihood of a cesarean section.

There are many obstetricians who do these versions, but most do not. Your doctor should know someone who has experience with this procedure.

During an external version, the baby's buttocks are lifted up out of the mother's pelvis, the baby's head is flexed, and the baby is then pushed into doing a forward somersault inside the uterus until its head is in the mother's pelvis. This is all done by abdominal manipulation. Sometimes, this is an extraordinarily easy procedure, especially with women who have had babies before.

The success rate of this procedure varies from doctor to doctor and also depends on whether or not the woman has had a baby before (a multipara).

Most experienced obstetricians can turn about 80 percent of babies of multiparas and about 50 percent of babies of primiparas (women who are having their first baby).

The risks are very low. The main thing that we worry about is umbilical cord compression or entanglement when the baby turns. If that happens, it will occur immediately, not two hours later or two days later. Cord compression leads to a sudden reduction in oxygen to the baby, and results in a dramatic and persistent drop in the baby's heart rate, down to about 60 or 70 beats per minute. Luckily, this rarely happens, but we watch for it by putting a fetal monitor on the mother after the version and observing for a while. Additionally, it is helpful to do an ultrasound after the version is completed to see that the cord does not end up being below the baby's head. Emergency cesareans for cord entanglement are rarely necessary. Sometimes, versions are not very easy, and in order to be successful, giving the mother medicine intravenously to relax the uterus (0.3 mg of Terbutaline) and to relax her and decrease pain (2 cc of Fentanyl) is very helpful. On occasion, epidural anesthesia is used to facilitate the version in those women who are exceptionally anxious and tense about any abdominal manipulations. Hypnosis may also help, since these difficult versions can be painful, especially if it is a first baby or if the mother is very anxious about it.

All in all, about two thirds of breech babies can be turned to a vertex position. About 90 percent of these babies stay head down and are delivered normally. Some of the most grateful patients are those whose babies have been turned.

They have avoided a probable cesarean section and they are happy, and their happiness makes our job a pleasant one.

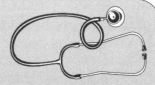

From the nurse's notes

Early in pregnancy, we often see babies in the breech position during an ultrasound. This is not a problem. In fact, even as late as 32 weeks, 90 percent of those babies who are in the breech position will turn around during the next several weeks and be delivered head first.

However, if you are getting to be about three to four weeks from your due date and your baby is known to be in a breech position, talk to your doctor about external version. If it is done successfully, you may save yourself the pain and aggravation of a cesarean section. Even if your baby cannot be turned, if it is in a frank breech position and your doctor is experienced in breech deliveries and your baby isn't too big for your pelvic bone structure, you can have your baby safely delivered vaginally.

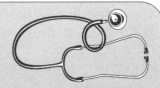

From the Doctor's Files

Years ago, it was not uncommon for a new baby to be named after the doctor who delivered him, but now it is pretty rare. It is fair to say that there are very few, if any, little Theodores running around Wisconsin because I delivered them into the world. I do, however, have a baby named after me, and it is a story I enjoy telling.

For a city of only 50,000, La Crosse has a surprisingly large population of the Hmong people, refugees from war-torn Laos. The vast majority of Hmong women do not speak English, and the cultural differences they face here are phenomenal.

Mai Xiong was such a woman, and I first saw her about one week before her due date with her first baby. Her baby was in the breech position and her doctor in the other main clinic in town had told her that she needed a cesarean because it was too dangerous to try a vaginal delivery.

Most Hmong people have a deep religious aversion to having surgery, and Mai was no exception. One of her friends told her that I had turned her baby for her, so Mai came to me, hoping that I could do the same for her. Unfortunately, I could not, because the baby was quite stuck in its position. However, using ultrasound, I could see that this baby was in the best possible breech position for a normal delivery, and I told her through an interpreter that I thought we should give it a try. Mai was excited about this option. So excited, in fact, that only three days later, she went into labor and was admitted to Lutheran Hospital to have her baby.

Her labor and delivery progressed smoothly, and, with only a little assistance from me, she gave birth to a healthy, six-pound, twelve-ounce baby boy, who came out buttocks first. From my point of view, she had delivered this baby the way it should have been delivered. From her point of view, by avoiding a cesarean section, her spiritual life had been saved.

The next morning, as I was about to make rounds, one of the nurses laughingly said, "Well, you finally had a baby named after you." I thought, "Theodore Xiong, what's so funny about that name?" I understood when I saw the baby's full name on the bassinet: "Peck Lutheran Xiong." I have never been so highly honored.

Appendix 1

Practicing relaxation for each practice session, the following procedure may be carried out:

1. The bladder should first be emptied, so that the pelvic muscles can be relaxed with safety. Then stand and stretch the whole body, breathing in deeply through the nose to full lung capacity. Then exhale, allowing the shoulders to drop and the head to fall forward as the lungs become empty.

2. Lie down on a wide couch, the floor, or a hard bed, with a pillow under your head and the upper part of your shoulders. Another pillow should be made into a roll and placed under your knees for support, so that both knee and hip joints are slightly bent.

3. The feet should be about six or eight inches apart. Arms flexed outward, the hands with palms down and fingers curled slightly inward. The head should be allowed to fall gently to one side on the pillow, with the chin slightly raised as the head falls back.

4. Take three or four slow deep breaths and, on breathing out each time, let every muscle in the body become limp and still. Think of the shoulders as "opening outward." Feel the arms hanging from the shoulders and the hands lying heavily on the bed. Fingers and thumbs must not move. There will be a sensation of sinking into, or even through, the bed. The feet fall outward upon the heels, and the knees are carried outward by the weight of the feet. There must be no movement of the toes.

5. The head and shoulders are to be so completely supported upon the pillow that the muscles of the neck are absolutely loose. Let the eyelids half close of their own weight.

6. Concentrate briefly on each arm without moving or tensing it, to be sure it is not being held stiffly in any part, that the muscles are not twitching or the fingers fidgeting. Do the same with the legs, buttocks, and back. Note carefully the muscles of the back. If they are relaxed, there will be a sensation of pressure upon the bed or floor from the weight of your body.

7. Relax the muscles of the face, the brow, eyelids, cheeks, and the muscles around the mouth. Think of your head as making a dent in the pillow. Particular care must be taken not to blink the eyes or move the eyeballs within their sockets. The muscles of the

face will be felt hanging loosely from the cheekbones, which causes the jaw to drop slightly and hang loose.

8. Release any remaining tension in the abdominal muscles
and pelvic floor muscles. Take two or three breaths deeply into the
diaphragm, letting the chest and abdominal wall collapse with its
own weight slowly as each breath is exhaled. Allow the breath to
leave the lungs through the mouth without controlling or impeding
it. Do not force it out. After each expiration, pause for two seconds
(or until you want a new breath) before inhaling into the
diaphragm again, deeply and gently. With each outgoing breath,
relax the abdominal wall more fully, and "let go" tension in the
pelvic muscles, as if opening up down below. Remember to keep
your lips parted and your cheeks and jaw "hanging loose," to help
relax the pelvic area. If your mouth is tense, you will be tensing the
pelvic area, too. As relaxation deepens, the breathing will become
very gentle and quiet, as if you were really asleep.

This perfectly smooth and almost imperceptible breathing is full
adequate to carry on all respiratory functions in labor during the
first stage, for less oxygen is needed during relaxation than when in
a state of tension or movement. It is not necessary to remain con-
scious of breathing once full relaxation is achieved.

9. Let all the joints of the body relax a little more with each outgoing breath until they seem to be detached altogether. Note the
train of sensations in the limbs---usually heaviness followed by light-
ness or "floating"; faint, transient pins and needles in the hands; feelings of warmth passing up from the extremities.

10. A pleasant, daydreaming state generally ensues (as in sun-
bathing) and any tendency to directed thinking should be deliber-
ately diverted into a daydream. Remain in this relaxed state for
about half an hour. (The sense of the passage of time is often lost
or blunted.) Sleep is not the aim, and for most patients muscular
relaxation without falling asleep seems to be more refreshing. But
relaxing again in this way at night will help many insomniacs put
themselves to sleep.

11. Get up slowly. Jumping up suddenly may cause faintness or
dizziness. Take two or three deep breaths, bend the knees and
arms once or twice, and then slowly sit up. Take two or three more
breaths before standing up. Stretch the body once more, and then
normal movement may again be safely resumed.

(From Childbirth Without Fear by Grandly Dick-Read p.80-82)

Appendix II

Diet for Gestational Diabetes

- You need the same healthy foods as other pregnant women.

- Gain a healthy amount of weight. The weight you gain depends on your weight before you were pregnant and the weight you have gained so far.

- It's OK to have foods and drinks sweetened with aspartame.

- Eat plenty of fruits, vegetables, and grains because they are healthy and help prevent constipation.

- Eat 3 small meals and 2 or 3 snacks spread out over the day. Don't skip meals or snacks.

- Eat a small breakfast. Blood sugar is most likely to be highest in the morning.

- Include foods high in Vitamins A and C daily (oranges, orange juice, potatoes, tomatoes, carrots, broccoli, strawberries, melons and bright-colored fruits and vegetables).

- Have foods high in iron every day—liver, kidney, shellfish, lean meat, poultry, fish, dried beans, green leafy vegetables, whole-grain and enriched breads and cereals, and fried fruits.

- Drink at least 8 cups of liquid a day (including milk).

Food Group	Servings	Serving Sizes
Grains Beans Starchy Vegetables	6 or more	1 slice bread 4 to 6 crackers 1 6-inch pancake 1/2 cup starchy vegetables 1/2 cup cooked pasta or rice 3/4 cup dry cereal 1 small potato
Vegetables	3 to 5	1 cup raw vegetables 1/2 cup cooked vegetables
Fruit	3 to 4	1 small fresh fruit 1/2 cup canned fruit or fruit juice
Milk	3 to 4	1 cup nonfat or low-fat milk or yogurt
Meat and Others	2 to 3	2 to 3 oz. cooked lean meat, poultry, or fish 2 to 3 oz. cheese 2 eggs 2 tbsp. Peanut butter
Fats and Sweets	Limit	Eat sweets seldom Use fats sparingly

Appendix III

Breastfeeding and the Use of Human Milk (RE9739)

AMERICAN ACADEMY OF PEDIATRICS (AAP) Policy Statement (excerpt) 1997

Recommended Breastfeeding Practices

1. Human milk is the preferred feeding for all infants, including premature and sick newborns, with rare exceptions. The ultimate decision on feeding of the infant is the mother's. Pediatricians should provide parents with complete, current information on the benefits and methods of breast-feeding to ensure that the feeding decision is a fully informed one. When direct breastfeeding is not possible, expressed human milk, fortified when necessary for the premature infant, should be provided. Before advising against breastfeeding or recommending premature weaning, the practitioner should weigh thoughtfully the benefits of breastfeeding against the risks of not receiving human milk.

2. Breastfeeding should begin as soon as possible after birth, usually within the first hour. Except under special circumstances, the newborn infant should remain with the mother throughout the recovery period. Procedures that may interfere with breastfeeding or traumatize the infant should be avoided or minimized.

3. Newborns should be nursed whenever they show signs of hunger, such as increased alertness or activity, mouthing, or rooting. Crying is a late indicator of hunger. Newborns should be nursed approximately 8 to 12 times every 24 hours until satiety, usually 10 to 15 minutes on each breast. In the early weeks after birth, nondemanding babies should be aroused to feed if 4 hours have elapsed since the last nursing. Appropriate initiation of breastfeeding is facilitated by continuous rooming-in. Formula evaluation of breastfeeding performance should be undertaken by trained observers and fully documented in the record during the first 24 to 48 hours after delivery and again at the early follow-up visit, which should occur 48 to 72 hours after discharge. Maternal recording of the time of each breastfeeding and its duration, as well as voidings and stoolings during the early days of breastfeeding in the hospital and at home, greatly facilitates the evaluation process.

4. No supplements (water, glucose water, formula, and so forth) should be given to breastfeeding newborns unless a medical indication exists. With sound breastfeeding knowledge and practices, supplements rarely are needed. Supplements and pacifiers should be avoided whenever possible and, if used at all, only after breastfeeding is well established.

5. When discharged <48 hours after delivery, all breastfeeding mothers and their newborns should be seen by a pediatrician or other knowledgeable health care practitioner when the newborn is 2 to 4 days of age. In addition to determination of infant weight and general health assessment, breastfeeding should be observed and evaluated for evidence of successful breastfeeding behavior. The infant should be assessed for jaundice, adequate hydration, and age-appropriate elimination patterns (at least six urinations per day and three to four stools per day) by 5 to 7 days of age. All newborns should be seen by 1 month of age.

6. Exclusive breastfeeding is ideal nutrition and sufficient to support optimal growth and development for approximately the first 6 months after birth. Infants weaned before 12 months of age should not receive cow's milk feedings but should receive iron-fortified infant formula. Gradual introduction of iron-enriched solid foods in the second half of the first year should complement the breast milk diet. It is recommended that breastfeeding continue for at least 12 months, and thereafter for as long as mutually desired.

7. In the first 6 months, water, juice, and other foods are generally unnecessary for breastfed infants. Vitamin D and iron may need to be given before 6 months of age in selected groups of infants (vitamin D for infants whose mothers are vitamin D-deficient or those infants not exposed to adequate sunlight; iron for those who have low iron stores or anemia). Fluoride should not be administered to infants during the first 6 months after birth, whether they are breast—or formula—fed. During the period from 6 months to 3 years of age, breastfed infants (and formula-fed infants) require fluoride supplementation only if the water supply is severely deficient in fluoride (<0.3 ppm).

8. Should hospitalization of the breastfeeding mother or infant be necessary, every effort should be made to maintain breastfeeding, preferably directly, or by pumping the breasts and feeding expressed breast milk, if necessary.

Appendix IV

The Mother-Friendly Childbirth Initiative

The First Consensus Initiative of the Coalition for Improving Maternity Services (CIMS)

Mission, Preamble and Principles

Mission

The Coalition for Improving Maternity Services (CIMS) is a coalition of individuals and national organizations with concern for the care and well-being of mothers, babies and families. Our mission is to promote a wellness model of maternity care that will improve birth outcomes and substantially reduce costs. This evidence-based mother, baby, and family-friendly model focuses on prevention and wellness as the alternatives to high-cost screening, diagnosis, and treatment programs.

Preamble

Whereas:

• In spite of spending far more money per capita on maternity and newborn care than any other country, the United States falls behind most industrialized countries in perinatal morbidity and mortality, and maternal mortality is four times greater for African-American women than for Euro-American women.

• Midwives attend the vast majority of births in those industrialized countries with the best perinatal outcomes, yet in the United States, midwives are the principal attendants at only a small percentage of births.

• Current maternity and newborn practices that contribute to high costs and inferior outcomes include the inappropriate

197

application of technology and routine procedures that are not based on scientific evidence.

- Increasing dependence on technology has diminished confidence in women's innate ability to give birth without intervention.

- The integrity of the mother-child relationship, which begins in pregnancy, is compromised by the obstetrical treatment of mother and baby as if they were separate units with conflicting needs.

- Although breastfeeding has been scientifically shown to provide optimum health, nutritional, and developmental benefits to newborns and their mothers, only a fraction of U.S. mothers are fully breastfeeding their babies by the age of six weeks.

- The current maternity care system in the United States does not provide equal access to health care resources for women from disadvantaged population groups, women without insurance, and women whose insurance dictates caregivers or place of birth.

Therefore,

We, the undersigned members of CIMS, hereby resolve to define and promote mother-friendly maternity services in accordance with the following principles:

Principles

We believe the philosophical cornerstones of mother-friendly care to be as follows:

Normalcy of the Birthing Process

- Birth is a normal, natural, and healthy process.

- Women and babies have the inherent wisdom necessary for birth.

- Babies are aware, sensitive human beings at the time of birth, and should be acknowledged and treated as such.

- Breastfeeding provides the optimum nourishment for new borns and infants.

- Birth can safely take place in hospitals, birth centers, and homes.

- The midwifery model of care, which supports and protects the normal birth process, is the most appropriate for the majority of women during pregnancy and birth.

Empowerment

- A women's confidence and ability to give birth and to care for her baby are enhanced or diminished by every person who gives her care, and by the environment in which she gives birth.

- A mother and baby are distinct yet interdependent during pregnancy, birth, and infancy. Their interconnected-ness is vital and must be respected.

- Pregnancy, birth, and the postpartum period are milestone events in the continuum of life. These experiences profoundly affect women, babies, fathers, and families, and have important and long-lasting effects on society.

Autonomy

Every woman should have the opportunity to:

- Have a healthy and joyous birth experience for herself and her family, regardless of her age or circumstances.

- Give birth as she wishes in an environment in which she feels nurtured and secure, and her emotional well-being, privacy, and personal preferences are respected.

- Have access to the full range of options for pregnancy, birth, and nurturing her baby, and to accurate information on all available birthing sites, caregivers, and practices.

199

- Receive accurate and up-to-date information about the benefits and risks of all procedures, drugs, and tests suggested for use during pregnancy, birth, and the postpartum period, with the rights to informed consent and informed refusal.

- Receive support for making informed choices about what is best for her and her baby based on her individual values and beliefs.

Do No Harm

- Interventions should not be applied routinely during pregnancy, birth, or the postpartum period. Many standard medical tests, procedures, technologies, and drugs carry risks to both mother and baby, and should be avoided in the absence of specific scientific indications for their use.

- If complications arise during pregnancy, birth, or the postpartum period, medical treatments should be evidence-based.

Responsibility

- Each caregiver is responsible for the quality of care she or he provides.

- Maternity care practice should be based not on the needs of the caregiver or provider, but solely on the needs of the mother and child.

- Each hospital and birth center is responsible for the periodic review and evaluation, according to current scientific evidence, of the effectiveness, risks, and rates of use of its medical procedures for mothers and babies.

- Society, through both its government and the public health establishment, is responsible for ensuring access to maternity services for all women, and for monitoring the quality of those services.

- Individuals are ultimately responsible for making informed choices about the health care they and their babies receive.

200

Index

205